ANATOMY PHYSIOLOGY
of
FEMALE REPRODUCTIVE SYSTEM

Useful for Medical, Nursing, Pharmacy and
other science faculties and Research

Dr. Pooja Soni Deol

BLUEROSE PUBLISHERS
India | U.K.

Copyright © Pooja Soni Deol 2023

All rights reserved by author. No part of this publication may be reproduced, stored in a retrieval system or transmitted in any form or by any means, electronic, mechanical, photocopying, recording or otherwise, without the prior permission of the author. Although every precaution has been taken to verify the accuracy of the information contained herein, the publisher assumes no responsibility for any errors or omissions. No liability is assumed for damages that may result from the use of information contained within.

BlueRose Publishers takes no responsibility for any damages, losses, or liabilities that may arise from the use or misuse of the information, products, or services provided in this publication.

For permissions requests or inquiries regarding this publication, please contact:

BLUEROSE PUBLISHERS
www.BlueRoseONE.com
info@bluerosepublishers.com
+91 8882 898 898
+4407342408967

ISBN: 978-93-5819-307-7

Cover design: Shivam
Typesetting: Namrata Saini

First Edition: August 2023

Foreword

Dr.Pooja Soni Deol has completed Ph.D (Nursing) In the department of Obstetrics & Gynecology Nursing . She has rich experience of more than 13 Years As a teacher & an Administrator. She has published articles In the National & International Journal & Presented Paper in National & International Conferences. She has been a resource person for Conferences & Workshops. She has an TNAI, Nursing Teacher Association,India Membership.

Dedication

I would like to dedicate this present book to my well-wishers & respected readers, I also dedicate this book to my supporting persons such as my parents, husband and my great mentor's.

The present book is especially dedicated to all Medical, Nursing, Pharmacy and other science faculties and Research

Acknowledgment

First and foremost, I would like to thank Almighty God for giving me the opportunity, ability, and knowledge to undertake this important task and to persevere and complete it satisfactorily.

I wish to avail myself of this opportunity to acknowledge a number of persons who have helped me at various stages in the pursuit of my research endeavour.

I would like to express my sincere gratitude to my parents, for giving me the opportunity to work in this area. It would never be possible for me to take this book to this level without his careful guidance, magnificent devotion, moral support, valuable suggestions, and providing materials, which has ever been a source of inspiration, to complete this book, it was an honor and privilege to work under his supervision.

The present work has been accomplished under the able co-supervision of my supportive seniors who, in spite of his busy schedule, rendered all support and help throughout the preparation of this work. His stimulating discussions, useful criticisms, and affectionate attitude have been a source of great inspiration for me. I, very enthusiastically and respectfully, offer my sincere thanks to them.

I must express my heartfelt gratitude to Blue Rose Publication Team, who motivated and initiated me into the subject. I was fortunate enough to have his valuable counsel, inspiring encouragement, and critical advice even after his moving abroad, without which it would have been rather very difficult for me to give the shape to the present work.

I shall be failing in my duty if I do not express here my deep sense of indebtedness to my parents, parent-in-law, and brothers-in-law especially without them continuous encouragement, enthusiastic support, rare sacrifices, and all-time financial help, it would not have been possible for me to devote so much time to complete my doctoral thesis and reach at this stage of my academic career. In fact, I do not find appropriate words to express my indebtedness for all that I have learned and got from them.

Preface

The course of human propagation is one that is both complex and fascinating. At the point when both the male and female conceptive systems are cooperating, they are answerable for the creation of new life. The interaction through which life forms make extra animals that are indistinguishable from themselves is called propagation. Nonetheless, rather than other substantial systems, the regenerative system isn't required for the endurance of an individual, in spite of the way that it is essential to the continuation of an animal categories. The organs that make up the female regenerative system are liable for the creation of female sex cells (generally called egg cells or ova), the transportation of these telephones to where they can be treated by sperm, the help of a climate that is useful for the advancement of the baby, and the conveyance of the embryo into the world once the hour of progress has reached a resolution. These organs additionally produce the female sex chemicals. The ovaries, Fallopian tubes, uterus, vagina, extra organs, and outside genital organs are all important for the female regenerative system.

This book has been divided into 6 chapters which is as follows –

CHAPTER – 1 INTRODUCTION

In the main section, an overall outline and idea of the female conceptive system have been examined. The pieces of the female conceptive system, like inward and outer parts, have been examined in this section. Further in this review, the functions of the female conceptive system have been momentarily talked about.

CHAPTER – 2 STRUCTURE OF FEMALE REPRODUCTIVE SYSTEM

In second section, we have examined an overall outline of the construction of the female regenerative system. The inward design, which comprises of the ovaries, fallopian cylinders, uterus, and vagina, has been talked about. Also, the outside design of the female conceptive system, which comprises of Mons Veneris, Labia Minora, Labia Majora, Vestibule, Clitoris, Skene's Organs,

Bartholin's Organ, Fourchette, Perineal Body, and Hymen, has been examined.

CHAPTER – 3 FUNCTIONS OF FEMALE REPRODUCTIVE SYSTEM

This part third is just in view of the elements of the female regenerative system. The elements of the vulva, vagina, uterus, fallopian cylinders, and ovaries have been talked about. Further, in this review, the job of the uterus has been introduced.

CHAPTER – 4 CONDITIONS AFFECTING THE FEMALE REPRODUCTIVE ORGANS

In this chapter 4th, we investigate the various conditions affecting female reproductive organisms, which have been discussed. The conditions that affect the reproductive organs are infections, uterine fibroids, endometriosis, polycystic ovary syndrome (PCOS), ovarian cysts and uterine polyps, cancers, and infertility.

CHAPTER – 5 FEMALE REPRODUCTIVE SYSTEM ANATOMY AND PHYSIOLOGY

In Section fifth, we talked about the female regenerative life structures through outside and inward female genitalia. Female regenerative physiology, alongside period, the feminine cycle, and the period cycle, have additionally been talked about. In this section, the Sexual Reaction Cycle and Ripeness, Female Physical and Physiological Brokenness, and Bosoms and Pelvis of the Female Regenerative System have been considered with their arrangement and capabilities.

CHAPTER – 6 CONCLUSION

In the last chapter 6th, the overall conclusion derived from the study is discussed.

Contents

Chapter – 1: Introduction 1
    1.1 Overview 1
    1.2 Concept of Female Reproductive System 4
    1.3 Parts of the Female Reproductive System 7
    1.4 How Does Reproduction Work? 21

Chapter – 2: Structure of Female Reproductive System 26
    2.1 Introduction 26
    2.2 Internal Structures 27
    2.3 External Structures 37

Chapter – 3: Functions of Female Reproductive System 46
    3.1 Main Functions of the Vulva 47
    3.2 Main Functions of the Vagina 48
    3.3 Main Functions of the Uterus 49
    3.4 Main Functions of the Fallopian Tubes 50
    3.5 Main Functions of the Ovaries 52
    3.6 The Role of the Uterus 53

Chapter – 4: Conditions Affecting the Female Reproductive Organs 55
    4.1 Infections 55
    4.2 Uterine Fibroids 64
    4.3 Endometriosis 68
    4.4 Polycystic Ovary Syndrome (PCOS) 71
    4.5 Ovarian Cysts and Uterine Polyps 73
    4.6 Cancers 76
    4.7 Infertility 79

Chapter – 5: Female Reproductive System Anatomy and Physiology 84
5.1 Female Reproductive Anatomy 85
5.2 Female Reproductive Physiology 89
5.3 Sexual Response Cycle and Fertility 108
5.4 Female Anatomical and Physiological Dysfunction 116
5.5 Breasts 122
5.6 Pelvis 131

Chapter – 6: Conclusion 135
References 139

CHAPTER - 1

Introduction

1.1 OVERVIEW

The start of embryogenesis is connoted by the course of preparation, which ordinarily happens in the fallopian tubes. The zygote will keep on isolating until it has delivered an enough number of ages of cells to shape a blastocyst, which will hence embed itself in the uterine wall. This denotes the start of the incubation stage, during which the incipient organism will keep on developing until it is conceived. Whenever the child has arrived where it can reside beyond the uterus, the cervix starts to widen, and the constrictions of the uterus help to move the baby through the birth trench (otherwise called the vagina).

Both the inside and outside sex organs of the female body are engaged with the course of propagation, spreading the word about up what is as the regenerative system of the female. In people, the female conceptive system is youthful upon entering the world and develops to complete development all through immaturity. This permits a lady to make gametes and convey a kid to full term. In different creatures, the female regenerative system is developed from birth. The vagina, the uterus, the fallopian tubes, and the ovaries are the sexual organs that are viewed as inside. The female regenerative system is powerless to diseases and is contained the vagina, the uterus, and the fallopian tubes. The vagina is the site of sexual development and birthing and is associated with the uterus at the cervix. The uterus, frequently known as the belly, is the organ that houses the undeveloped organism before it develops into the child. Also, the uterus produces discharges that work with the development of sperm to the fallopian tubes. It is in these cylinders that sperm can treat the ova (egg cells) that are produced by the ovaries. The labia, clitoris, and vaginal entry are instances of the outside sexual organs, which are likewise alluded to as the privates. Private parts are one more name for the outside sex organs. An ovum is delivered by the ovaries over the span of the period. This ovum then goes down the fallopian tube and into the uterus. On the off chance that sperm and egg cells impact when an egg is on the way to the uterus, a solitary sperm cell might have the option to enter the egg cell and treat it, bringing about the development of a zygote.

The parts of the female conceptive system that are at present the most significant and cutting-edge The pieces of the body that are straightforwardly involved are not a lot and incorporate the ovary, fallopian tubes, uterus, vagina, outside genitalia, and bosoms (albeit the bosoms won't be canvassed in this article). In any case, for the conceptive system to work appropriately, it should be composed with countless different systems all through the body. Our examination will focus solely on the designs and elements of the parts that are straightforwardly connected with the female conceptive system, with just a little measure of consideration paid to the helper systems. We start with the introduction of the gross life structures, then happen to the histological life structures, and afterward finish up with the physiology. If one has any desire to have a total cognizance of the female regenerative system, fathoming each of the three aspects is important. If we somehow happened to take a gander at this according to a clinical viewpoint, we would likewise need to incorporate organic chemistry, pathophysiology, and pharmacology; nonetheless, there are an extraordinary number of other benevolent acts that could be used all things being equal assuming this more thorough view is wanted.

The expression "regenerative system" alludes to the assortment of organs in the body that are liable for the production of kids. To have the option to survey the soundness of these systems, to advance conceptive system wellbeing, to really focus on conditions that could influence the regenerative organs, and to give client instruction concerning the regenerative system, medical caretakers need to have an exhaustive comprehension of the life structures and physiology of the male and female conceptive systems. This talk gives an outline of the conceptive systems of all kinds of people, as well as the monthly cycle and how it relates to generation.

Although the end goal of the human reproductive system is to generate children, the more immediate goals of this system are to provide pleasure and to encourage the formation of social bonds. This may be observed in our closest cousins, the bonobo chimpanzees, who engage in sexual behavior for a broad range of reasons in addition to the production of children. These reasons include experiencing pleasure, strengthening bonds, and relieving stress. A group of organs inside an organism that function as a unit in order to create children is referred to as the reproductive system or the genital system. Important components of the reproductive system include a wide variety of non-living substances, including as fluids, hormones, and pheromones. In contrast to the majority of organ systems, the reproductive systems of distinct species often exhibit substantial diversity. Because of these differences, it is possible for the genetic material of two people to be combined, and as a result, there is a probability that the child will have a higher genetic fitness.

The male and female conceptive systems are to sustain the human species by creating youngsters. This is achieved by means of multiplication. That might appear to be dry and unoriginal from the start, however assuming that we remember that everybody of us is a continuation of our animal varieties and that a considerable lot of us will have our own organic posterity. In spite of the fact that there are different types of creatures that give parental consideration to their youngsters as coordinated families or social orders, the human species is extraordinary in how much consideration that people commit to proliferation and to everyday life due to the social factors that shape our general public.

Nonetheless, especially like various creatures, human life designs and physiology assume a part in the real creation of youths as well as their improvement throughout the span of time. Both the male and female regenerative systems are answerable for the creation of gametes, generally called sperm and egg cells, as well as the assistance of the association of gametes during the treatment cycle that follows sexual development. At the point when a lady is pregnant, the undeveloped organism or child keeps on developing inside the lady's uterus until it is sufficiently experienced to have the option to live beyond the belly.

The conceptive organs and the capabilities that every one serves, whether it be currently creating new life or in the general situation of the regenerative system overall. To begin, nonetheless, we will discuss how gametes are framed.

1.2 CONCEPT OF FEMALE REPRODUCTIVE SYSTEM

Interior and outside organs cooperate to make up the female conceptive system. This interaction is liable for the development of chemicals as well as richness, feminine cycle, and sexual movement.

1.2.1 What Is the Female Reproductive System?

The parts that make up a woman's reproductive system are as per the following: a single uterus, fallopian tubes, paired ovaries, a vagina, and external genital tissues. The ovaries are liable for the creation of egg cells, also known as ova, which then make their way to the uterus through the fallopian tubes. The embryo-fetus will foster within the mother's uterus while it is there.

The female reproductive system comprises of the components of the body that assist women and people who are designated female upon entering the world (AFAB) in the following ways:

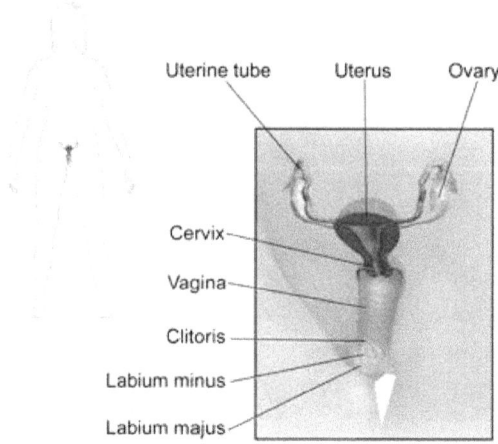

Figure 1.1 Female Reproductive Systems

Have sexual intercourse: - The inclusion and pushing of the penis into the vagina with the end goal of sexual delight, multiplication, or both is an illustration of the sexual activity known as sex, otherwise called sex or sex. This movement is likewise alluded to as vaginal sex and vaginal intercourse. Different kinds of penetrative sex incorporate fingering (sexual entrance by the fingers), butt-centric sex (infiltration of the rear-end by the penis), oral sex (infiltration of the mouth by the penis or oral entrance of the female genitalia), oral entrance of the female genitalia, and oral entrance of the male genitalia), and oral entrance using a dildo (particularly a tie on dildo). These exercises incorporate actual closeness between at least two people and are frequently utilized principally among people to accomplish either physical or profound joy. They may likewise add to the improvement of human bonds.

There are different points of view on what is sex or different types of sexual movement, and these points of view might affect individuals' opinion on sexual wellbeing. Albeit penile-vaginal entrance and the possibility of making descendants are much of the time individuals' thought process of when they hear "sex," explicitly the expression "copulation," the term is additionally broadly used to allude to penetrative oral sex and penile-butt-centric sex, particularly the last option. It frequently alludes to sexual movement that includes entrance, while non-entering sexual action is known as "outercourse." Notwithstanding, non-infiltrating sexual action might in any case be viewed as sex. Any kind of sexual movement might be alluded to as "sex," which is many times utilized as a shorthand for "sex." In light of the fact that partaking in these exercises seriously endangers people of getting physically sent diseases (STIs), safe sexual practices are supported by wellbeing specialists to restrict the probability of contamination transmission.

Certain sexual works on, including interbreeding, sex with kids, prostitution, assault, zoophilia, homosexuality, early and extramarital sex, and zoophilia, are restricted in various overall sets of laws across the world. Individual decisions about sex or other sexual way of behaving, like choices about virginity, as well as decisions in regards to the law and public arrangement may likewise be impacted by strict perspectives. Despite the fact that there are consistent ideas, for example, the restriction of infidelity, strict points of view on sexuality might shift considerably starting with one strict practice or gathering then onto the next, even inside a similar strict custom.

It is more common to refer to the reproductive sexual intercourse between non-human animals as "copulation," and during this process, sperm may be transferred into the reproductive OP of the female.

Female gametes emerge from microbe cells. In the uterus, oogonia partition rapidly, and by the seventh month of pregnancy, there are around 7 million microbe cells present. After this, there is a sharp drop in the all out number of microorganism cells; most of oogonia vanish, and the cells that are left, essential oocytes, start the principal meiotic division. These cells quit separating at the prophase I stage and remain lethargic until the female conceptive time of menarche. Every oocyte is encircled by an early stage follicle that is made out of granulosa cells and theca cells. At the point when early stage follicles arrive at their development stage, the granulosa cells that encompass the egg start to duplicate and shape concentric layers. The oocyte goes through a cycle that outcomes in a critical expansion in its volume. The beginning of menarche is set apart by the occasional resumption of meiosis by discrete gatherings of oocytes, which permits advancement to continue. Oocytes are trapped in the metaphase II stage just around when they get treated. When delivering its second polar body, the oocyte changes into an ovum, and the course of meiosis restarts once the egg is initiated by a sperm cell, which is a male gamete.

- **Reproduce**

The age of relatives is generation. Abiogenetic propagation and sexual proliferation are the two essential sorts. An animal that duplicates physically integrates the hereditary material from both of its folks and is hereditarily unmistakable. Abiogenetic propagation makes hereditarily indistinguishable children by having one parent recreate itself.

The major and helper sex organs are all essential for the female conceptive system. The significant sex organs in females are two ovaries, which likewise discharge female sex chemicals remembering progesterone and estrogen for expansion to creating ova or eggs. The uterus, fallopian cylinders, cervix, and vagina are among the other embellishment sex organs. The labia minora, labia majora, and clitoris make up the outside genitalia. In spite of not being viewed as genital organs, the mammary organs are huge organs in the female conceptive system.

- **Menstruate**

The covering of your uterus sheds every month during period. Menses, feminine period, monthly cycle, and period are different names for period. Feminine blood, which is comprised of a combination of blood and tissue from your uterus, leaves your body by means of your vagina subsequent to leaving your uterus.

Chemicals control the beginning of period. Your body involves chemicals as compound couriers. At specific minutes all through your feminine cycle, your ovaries, a part of your regenerative system, and your pituitary organ, situated in your mind, produce and delivery explicit chemicals.

The covering of uterus becomes thicker because of these chemicals. This happens so an egg might embed into your uterine coating in case of a pregnancy. Your ovaries discharge an egg (ovulation) because of chemicals. The egg ventures by means of your fallopian cylinders and hangs tight for sperm there. Pregnancy can't happen on the off chance that a sperm doesn't prepare that egg.

1.3 PARTS OF THE FEMALE REPRODUCTIVE SYSTEM

The outside and inside parts that make up the female conceptive life systems are both present.

1.3.1 External Parts

The designs that are situated around the vaginal entry and those that are outside to the hymen, which is the film that traverses the vaginal opening, are altogether alluded to as the female outer genitalia. The mons pubis, generally called the mons veneris, the labia majora and minora, the clitoris, the vestibule of the vagina, the bulb of the vestibule, and the greater vestibular organs are the physical plans that make up the vestibule of the vagina.

The mons pubis is the adjusted distinction that may be tracked down before the pubic symphysis. Shaped by greasy tissue is tracked down under the skin. In youth, there may be several fine hairs; later, all through pubescence, they will become harsher and more abundant. In outset, there may be several fine hairs. The level line that coincidentally finds the lower waist implies the top uttermost reaches of the ragged district. The labia majora are two prominent folds of skin that dive and aft from the mons pubis to join the skin of the perineum. They are situated on each side of the pubic bone. They make up the horizontal farthest reaches of the vulval or pudendal separated, which is the area that is liable for getting the openings of the vagina and the urethra. Within surface of each and every labium is smooth yet contains sebaceous organs, however the external surface of each and every labium is pigmented and covered with hairs. The labia majora are home to sweat organs as well as greasy and connective tissue that is free. They incorporate tissue that is comparative in appearance to the dartos muscle and associate with the scrotum in folks. The round ligament (for additional data, see beneath) The uterus is made sure to end in the tissue of the labium. The labia minora are two little creases of skin that contain no greasy tissue and expand aft on either side of the section into the vagina. These folds are situated on each side of the part into the vagina. They are around 4 centimeters (around 1.5 inches) long and are situated inside the labia majora. An upper piece of each and every labium short creases over the clitoris, the plan in the female that compares to the penis (without the urethra) in the male, to convey a crease called the prepuce of the clitoris, and a lower portion folds under the clitoris to frame its frenulum. These folds are situated toward the front of the female regenerative system. A crease that interfaces the two labia minora at the back across the midline is reached out during conveyance. This overlay is known as the labia minora overlap. Albeit the labia minora don't have hair, they really have organs that produce sebum and sweat.

A little erectile design known as the clitoris is comprised of two corpora cavernosa that are isolated from each other by a parcel. It has a delicate place of light erectile tissue known as the glans clitoridis, which is to some extent covered behind the front finishes of the labia minora. The external gap of the urethra is situated around 2.5 centimeters (around 1 inch) behind the clitoris and straightforwardly before the kickoff of the vaginal channel.

The gap that is framed between the labia minora and fills in as the entry to both the urethra and the vagina is known as the vestibule of the vagina. The hymen vaginae is a shaky overlap of mucous film that might take on a wide range of structures and is situated close to the entry of the vagina. Following the break of the hymen, the extras of the hymen, which are minimal circular ascents, are alluded to as the carunculae hymenales. The bulb of the vestibule, which is intently resembling the bulb of the penis, involves two stretched masses of erectile tissue that lay one on each side of the vaginal section. These masses resemble the penis bulb. More significant vestibular organs are minimal mucous organs that open through a channel in the split between the hymen and each labium short. These organs are situated at the back farthest points of the labial appendages. They are what could be compared to the bulbourethral organs found in guys. The blood supply and nerve supply that are given to the female outside genital organs are very tantamount to those that are given to the similar to tissues in the male body.

The outside parts of your genitalia fill two needs: they safeguard the inside organs from tainting and empower sperm to get to the female regenerative lot. The aggregate word for your outside private parts is all vulva, which alludes to your own vulva. There is a typical misguided judgment that "vagina" might be utilized to allude to all parts of female proliferation. Then again, your vagina is a different construction that is tracked down inside your body.

Your vulva, or external genitalia, consists mostly of:

- **Labia majora**: The other exterior conceptive organs are contained and protected by the labia majora, which literally translates to "enormous lips." As a person goes through the pubescent process, new hair begins to grow in the outer layer of the labia majora, which also has organs that produce sweat and oil. The labia majora are two enormous longitudinal folds of skin that extend from the mons pubis to the perineum. They are frequently referred to as the labium majus (solitary: labium majus). They disseminated information regarding what are known as the vulva's labia alongside the labia minora. Physically, the labia majora resemble a man's scrotum. The labia majora are two enormous longitudinal folds of skin that extend from the mons pubis to the perineum. They are frequently referred to as the labium majus (solitary: labium majus). They shared information regarding what are known as the vulva's labia alongside the labia minora. Physically, the labia majora resemble a man's scrotum. They start with the labioscrotal folds, viewed from an embryological perspective. This demonstrates that they develop in male infants from the same previously physically undifferentiated physical tissue as the scrotum, the pack of skin found beneath the penis in males. In the first trimester of pregnancy, the scrotum develops in females using a similar architecture.

- Other male and female regenerative organs follow a similar course of sex separation (see List of Related Male and Female Conceptive Organs), with some organs of the sexes having comparable but not identical designs and functions (such as the balls, which contain male gonads and female ovaries, similar to male and female urethras, erectile corpus cavernosum penis and prepuce in the penis (prepuce), and the corpus caver Anyhow, some male and female genital parts, such as the inner female genitalia, develop into structures that are entirely distinct from one another. There are important equals and crucial divergences brought about by the development of the scrotum and labia majora. The labia majora, like the scrotum, may develop a hazier variation than the skin above them after pubescence. The female privates in the preceding photographs have been shaved so that their shape may be seen more clearly. The labia majora, like the scrotum, may also sprout pubic hair on their exterior surface. The two labia majora and the pudendal divide between them are formed by the labioscrotal folds in males, which generally merge lengthwise in the center to form a sack for the male balls (gonads) to drop into from the pelvis. This takes place as the embryo is being sexually separated. The development of the labia majora may seem more direct since it only consists of greasy tissue covered in skin, but because female balls (ovaries) do not descend from the pelvis, it very well may have less of an impact on the functioning of the female body as a whole than the scrotum with gonads does for men. There may be a piece or edge on the scrotum that was dropped after the combo interaction. The male and female genitalia may occasionally display all the telltale signs of being ambiguous for either sexual orientation. This can arise when the phallus is too big for a clitoris but too small for a standard penis, the outside urethral opening is in an unusual location, and the labia and scrotum are totally or partially fused but lack movable balls. However, there are some instances where healthy male children may be born with their balls truly attached to their bodies.

- **Labia minora**: the "little lips," also known as the labia minora, can come in a variety of shapes and sizes. They are immediately discovered in your labia majora, covering the openings to your vagina and urethra. Your urethra is the tube that carries urine from your bladder to the outside of your body, and your vagina is the passageway that connects the lower portion of your uterus to the outside of your body. Since this skin is so sensitive, it could easily get inflamed and swollen. The labia minora (Latin for 'more modest lips,' solitary: labium less) are two folds of skin that are essential for the human vulva. They expand outwards from the vaginal and urethral openings to encase the vestibule. Different names for the labia minora incorporate the internal labia, inward lips, vaginal lips, and nymphae. These labia are situated in the space between the labia majora, in some cases known as the "bigger lips." There is an expansive scope of variety in the size, variety, and type of the labia minora between people. In females, the labia minora are physically like the urethral surface of the penis in guys.

- **Clitoris**: Your clitoris is a little, delicate distension that is much the same as a penis in males or the people who were assigned male at birth

(AMAB). It is located where your two labia minora meet. Your clitoris is extremely delicate to stimulation and is safeguarded by a fold of skin known as the prepuce, which covers it. The clitoris is a female genital organ that is found in ostriches, vertebrates, and a chosen handful different types of creatures. It very well might be articulated by the same token. The region that is apparent in people is known as the glans, and it is located simply over the entry of the urethra and at the front intersection of the labia minora (internal lips). Since it does exclude the distal area (or opening) of the urethra like the penis, which is the male homologue (same) to the clitoris, it isn't used for urination. The penis is the male homologue (same) to the clitoris. In by far most of creatures, the clitoris has no regenerative reason. Albeit the clitoris is involved by not very many creatures for urination or propagation, the spotted hyena, which has an extraordinarily enormous clitoris, is one of the exemptions. This species can urinate, mate, and conceive an offspring through the clitoris. There are a couple of different sorts of creatures that likewise have a major clitoris, for example, lemurs and bug monkeys. The clitoris is the most delicate erogenous zone in human females and is generally viewed as the major actual wellspring of sexual delight in human females. A distension in the undeveloped organism known as the genital tubercle leads to its improvement in creatures like people and different vertebrates. The tubercle is at first undifferentiated; notwithstanding, all through the improvement of the regenerative system, it will develop into either a penis or a clitoris relying upon the quantity of androgens (which are generally male chemicals) that it is presented to. This not set in stone by the orientation of the person. The clitoris is a complex design that differs with regards to the two its size and its level of responsiveness. It is trusted that the glans (top) of the human clitoris has 8,000, and most likely considerably more than 10,000, touchy sensitive spots. The glans is about the size and state of a pea.

The clitoris has been the subject of conversation in fields, for example, sexology, medication, and brain science and it has likewise been the subject of social constructionist examinations and investigations. These debates incorporate a wide assortment of points, including anatomical accuracy, orientation disparity, female genital mutilation, orgasmic causes, and their physiological explanation for the Sweet spot. Regardless of the way that the sole known capability of the clitoris in people is to offer sexual delight, whether the clitoris is minimal, an adaptation, or plays a conceptive part has been the subject of much contention. The social originations of the clitoris remember the significance of its job for female sexual delight, suppositions about its veritable size and profundity, and varying attitudes towards genital alteration, for example, clitoris augmentation, clitoris penetrating, and clitoridectomy. Genital alteration might be performed for different reasons, including corrective, clinical, or social ones. How clitoris is depicted in various societies has a significant bearing on the way things are known and perceived. Studies recommend that information on its presence and anatomy is restricted in contrast with that of other sexual organs, and that more education about it could assist with alleviating social marks of shame associated with the female body and female sexual delight. A portion of these marks of disgrace remember the convictions that the clitoris and vulva for general are outwardly unappealing, that female masturbation is inappropriate, or that men ought normal to dominate and control ladies' climaxes.

- **Vaginal opening**: The vaginal trench creates an aperture that allows your body's female blood and unborn children to depart. Some items that might enter your vagina through the opening in your vagina include tampons, fingers, sex toys, or penises. Prior to the vaginal aperture, which is situated at the rear finish of the vulval vestibule, lies the urethral gap. The entrance to the vagina is often covered by the labia minora, commonly known as the vaginal lips. However, after a vaginal birth, this opening might become apparent. The hymen is a very thin layer of mucosal tissue that either completely surrounds the vaginal entrance or just covers it in part. The hymen may experience a wide range of changes as a result of sexual activity and giving birth. It is possible for it to totally vanish where it has been broken, or it may leave behind fragments known as carunculae myrtiformes. In such case, because to its high degree of elasticity, it may return to its original position. In addition, the hymen may get lacerated as a result of illness, injury, medical examination, masturbation, or physical activity. Because of these factors, the virginity of a woman cannot be verified with absolute certainty by inspecting the hymen.

- **Hymen**: One of the pieces of tissue that covers or surrounds a portion of your vaginal entrance is called the hymen. It comes into existence throughout development and is already there at birth. The hymen is a little piece of mucosal tissue that wraps around or partly covers the external vaginal entrance. It is also known as the hymenal ring. It is comparable in anatomy to the vagina and is a component of the vulva, which is another name for the external genitalia. Although the hymen may take on a variety of forms, it most often takes on a crescent-shaped look in children. Estrogen is responsible for the changes in appearance and increased elasticity of the hymen that occur throughout puberty. The post-pubertal hymen may take on a variety of normal forms, ranging from thin and elastic to thick and somewhat hard, depending on the individual. In very unusual cases, it could be totally missing.

It is possible for the hymen to rupture or tear during the initial penetrative interaction, which often results in discomfort and, in rare cases, modest transient bleeding or spotting. There is a variety of information on the frequency of ripping or bleeding following the first sexual encounter. The presence or absence of the hymen as a sign of virginity is not a reliable indication. Despite the fact that "virginity testing" is still a widespread practice in certain cultures, surgical repair of the hymen is occasionally performed alongside the test in order to provide the impression of virginity. It is possible for hymen injuries of a lesser severity to heal on their own without the need for surgical intervention. The genital plot creates all through embryogenesis, starting in the third seven day stretch of pregnancy and going on through the subsequent trimester. The hymen is delivered after the vagina, which happens during the third seven day stretch of pregnancy. The urorectal septum starts to create at week seven of pregnancy and allotments the rectum from the urogenital sinus. At the finish of the 10th week, the Mullerian conduits have moved far enough descending to arrive at the urogenital sinus, so, all in all they have shaped the uterovaginal waterway and embedded themselves into the sinus. At the finish of the twelfth week, the Mullerian channels consolidate to shape the unaleria, an early type of the uterovaginal trench. At the finish of the fifth month, the vaginal canalization is done, and the fetal hymen is created from the proliferation of the sinovaginal bulbs. Here the Mullerian conduits meet the urogenital sinus. The fetal hymen for the most part perforates previously or not long after conveyance.

The innervation of the hymen is rather extensive. In new-born infants, the hymen is thick, light pink, and redundant (folds in on itself and may protrude). This is because the infants are still subject to the hormonal impact of their mothers. This impact is maintained during the first two to four years of a new-born's life by hormones that are produced by the infant. Their hymenal aperture is often in the form of an annulus (circumferential opening). Following the neonatal stage, the diameter of the hymenal aperture (as measured inside the hymenal ring) increases by roughly one millimeter for each year of age beyond the neonatal stage. At the time of puberty, estrogen causes the hymen to transform into a structure that is very elastic and fibrous.

- **Opening to your urethra**: The hole in your body through which urine exits is the entrance to your urethra. Urine is expelled from the bodies of females and men via a tube called the urethra, which gets its name from the Greek word oeourthra. This cylinder interfaces the urinary bladder to the urinary meatus and is known as the urethra. In human females and different primates, the urethra associates with the pee meatus over the vagina. Notwithstanding, in marsupial females, the urethra exhausts into the urogenital sinus rather than the urinary meatus over the vagina. Urination is the sole capability of a female's urethra, while ejaculation and urination are both done by men by means of their urethras. The outside urethral sphincter is a striated muscle that empowers an individual to regulate their pee on their own will. The sympathetic division of the autonomic sensory system supplies nerves to the inside sphincter, which is created by the compulsory smooth muscles that line the bladder neck and urethra. The inner sphincter controls the progression of pee from the bladder into the urethra. Neither men nor females are brought into the world without an inside sphincter in their anatomy.

1.3.2 Internal Parts

The female reproductive organs that are housed internally inside the pelvic cavity are referred to as the internal genitalia.

"Genitalia" alludes to either the female or male conceptive organs. There are both apparent and inward designs that make up the genitalia. The male outer genitalia comprise of the balls, or scrotum, and the penis. The clitoris, labia minora, and labia majora, also referred to as the vulva, make up the female outer genitalia. Along with the fallopian cylinders and ovaries, the female internal genitalia also includes the vagina, cervix, uterus, and ovaries. The components of the male internal genitalia are the vas deferens, epididymis, and testicles.

The female regenerative system, normally alluded to as the female inward genitalia, might be tracked down inside the pelvic hole of a human female.

The female regenerative system is engaged with the cycles of becoming pregnant, considering a youngster, and conceiving an offspring.

The reproductive system is also responsible for a substantial impact on other parts of the body's health. For example, the ovaries are responsible for producing hormones that have an effect not just on mood but also on cholesterol levels, bone density, and cardiovascular health.

- **Vagina:** Your vagina is a solid channel that interfaces the cervix, which is the base part of the uterus, to the beyond your body. This is fundamental for the course of childbirth. It can extend to give space to a child during birth and afterward agreement to the size important to convey something as slim as a tampon. It is coated with mucous films, which add to its capacity to hold dampness. The vagina is a fibromuscular (made up of tough, stringy tissue) trench that extends from the cervix of the uterus or belly to the outside of the body. This suggests that the tissue of the vagina is both robust and stringy. The treated egg goes through the cervix and into the uterus to start the course of pregnancy. It is every now and again alluded to as the birth channel when individuals are discussing the system that happens during pregnancy. At the point when a couple participates in sexual movement, the vagina grows to give space to the male genital organs to enter. The male ejaculates spermatozoa-containing sperm into the vagina of the female during the demonstration of climax, which might bring about the fertilization of the egg cell, ordinarily known as the ovum.

- **Cervix:** The cervix is the lowest portion of the uterus that you have. Sperm are able to pass through the opening in the centre, whereas menstrual blood is able to depart. During a vaginal delivery, your cervix will soften and dilate, which will make it possible for your baby to exit your body. The cervix is what stops items like tampons and other feminine hygiene products from getting lost within your body. The uterus connects with the upper section of the vagina at a lower, slenderer portion known as the cervix. This is where a woman gives birth. The "neck" of the uterus is the location of this organ. Possibly it is tube shaped in structure or it is situated towards the lateral walls of the pelvic depression. Either is valid. These organs are the ones that are liable for the development of chemicals as well as the generation of egg cells, otherwise called ova. Egg cells are otherwise called ova.

The course of ovulation alludes to the cycle wherein the egg cell, otherwise called the ovum, is set free from the ovary. The recurrence of ovulation, which fluctuates consistently and is straightforwardly associated to the length of a lady's period, is a significant figure deciding if a lady will get pregnant. Following ovulation, the egg cell will make its way to the uterus through the Fallopian tube; however, it will ultimately be swallowed up by the Fallopian tube once it reaches the uterus. Occasionally, a sperm cell will arrive after the egg cell has already begun its trip and fertilize the egg. It is the egg cell's job to release certain chemicals that are required for guiding the sperm, and it is also the egg cell's job to make it possible for the surface of the egg to link to the surface of the sperm. The egg cell is an essential component in the process of fertilization. The process of fertilization may begin after the egg has finished ingesting the sperm and is ready to accept them.

- **Uterus**: During pregnancy, the child is held inside the uterus, which is an empty organ as a pear. The cervix and the corpus are the two parts that make up your uterus separately. During pregnancy, the corpus of your uterus, which is the greater piece of the organ, increases. the uterus, otherwise called the belly, is a solid organ of the female regenerative system that is put between the bladder and the rectum. It has the type of an altered pear. It is responsible for providing nutrition and a safe environment for a fertilized egg until the time comes for the fetus, also known as the offspring, to be delivered.

- **Ovaries**: Your ovaries are a couple of minuscule organs that have an oval shape and are situated on each side of your uterus. Eggs and chemicals are both delivered by your ovaries. The ovaries are a couple of oval designs that are located on each side of the uterus in the pelvic depression. Their length is around four centimeters. The wide tendon is an overlay of the peritoneum that covers the ovaries, though the ovarian tendon is an overlap of the peritoneum that runs from the average side of an ovary to the mass of the uterus. These ligaments have a role in maintaining the ovaries in their proper position. Primary follicles are those that are present at birth and may be found inside an ovary. There are several hundred thousand of them. Only 300 to 400 of these follicles will develop mature eggs throughout the years when a woman is fertile enough to birth children. As is the case with the production of sperm in males, the quantity of potential gametes much exceeds what is really required; yet, this helps guarantee that the human species will continue to exist.

The morphologic differences that exist in a lady's bosoms' size, shape, volume, tissue thickness, pectoral localization, and separating, as well as how they appear and feel, are liable for deciding the natural structure, pectoral situation, and dispersing of her bosoms. This incorporates how they show up and feel. There is no association between the size of a lady's bosoms and the extent of fat to drain organs found in her bosom tissue, nor is there an association between the size of a lady's bosoms and her ability to nurture a youngster. Both the size and the state of the bosoms might be impacted by hormonal changes that happen naturally during an individual's life expectancy, (for example, during pubescence, menstruation, pregnancy, and menopause), as well as by ailments, (for example, virginal bosom hypertrophy). For instance, all through immaturity, a lady's body goes through a progression of changes that incorporate menstruation, pregnancy, and menopause. The natural state of the not set in stone to some degree by the help given by the suspensory Cooper's tendons, the fundamental muscle and bone designs of the chest, as well as the skin envelope. The suspensory tendons keep the bosom fastened to the clavicle (collarbone) and the clavico-pectoral belt (which interfaces the collarbone to the chest), the two of which are associated with one another by the clavico-pectoral sash. These tendons go through and encompass the tissues of the bosom's fat and milk organs. The skin envelope is what gives the bosom its structure and is answerable for guaranteeing that it keeps on having that structure over the span of one's lifetime. The chest wall is answerable for the situating, attachment, and backing of the bosom. Most of ladies have a natural propensity for one of their bosoms to be impressively bigger than the other. Dependent upon one fourth, everything being equal, will encounter an unevenness of the bosoms that isn't just more self-evident yet additionally more steady over the long haul. Specialists have recognized four essential drivers of bosom hanging in ladies: smoking cigarettes, the quantity of pregnancies a lady has had, gravity, and fluctuations in her weight both when pregnancy. Despite the way that a broadly considered conviction breastfeeding is liable for hanging bosoms, research has shown that this isn't exactly the situation. The association between the lower part of each bosom and the chest is made by the profound sash, which is located over the pectoralis significant muscles and runs down the length of the chest. Due to a district known as the retromammary space, the bosom can move. This space might be found between the chest wall and the pectoralis significant muscle. The chest (thoracic depression) dynamically slants outward in an outward course from the thoracic delta, which is situated on top of the breastbone, and upwards to the most reduced ribs that help the bosoms. This happens toward a path out from the focal point of the body. The inframammary crease, frequently alluded to as the IMF or the least most expansion of the anatomic bosom, is a trademark that is created anatomically when the bosom skin sticks to the basic connective tissues of the chest. Different names for the inframammary crease incorporate the IMF and the least most augmentation of the anatomic bosom. Where the base piece of the bosom associates with the chest, you will actually want to see this trademark. It is normal practice to describe the surface of typical bosom tissue as having the sensation of being nodular or granular; by and by, the degree to which this is actually the case might change a seriously little starting with one lady then onto the next.

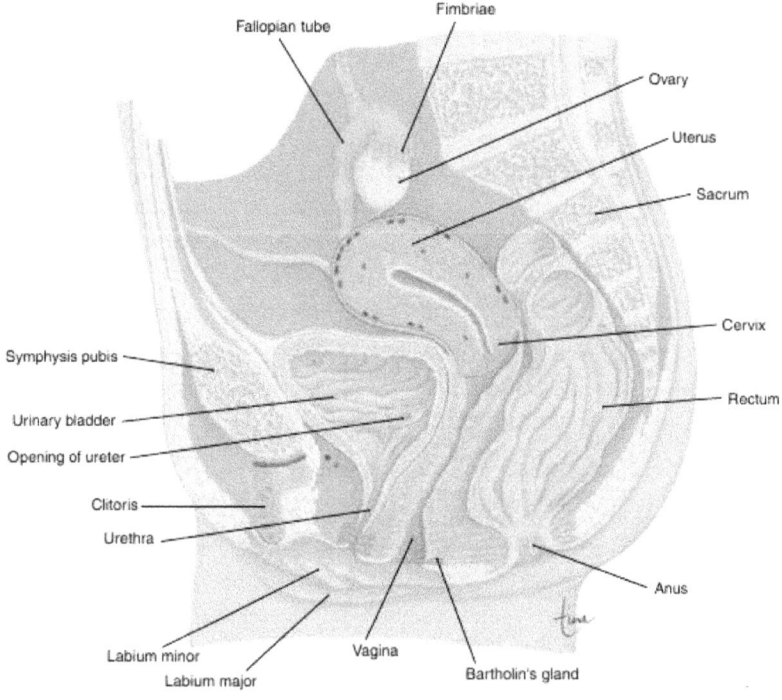

Figure 1.2: Female reproductive system shown in a midsagittal section through the pelvic cavity

An oocyte is a cell that has the potential to mature into an ovum or egg, and the main follicles of the ovary each contain one of these cells. Oocytes are found in female reproductive organs. The follicle cells, which are the cells that make estrogen and are spread all over the area surrounding the oocyte, may be found in the follicle. These cells are located around the oocyte. We spoke about the maturation of a follicle, which is a process that requires FSH and estrogen, in the part that was just before the one that was devoted to the process of oogenesis. This section was immediately before the one that was dedicated to the process of oogenesis. Ovulation happens because of the front pituitary organ emitting a chemical known as luteinizing chemical (LH), which regulates the monthly cycle. Ovulation is the cycle wherein the ovum is removed from the body after the break of the mature follicle, and the name "ovulation" alludes to this interaction. In specific quarters, a mature follicle is otherwise called a graafian follicle. This is a more specialized term. At this point, the improvement of some further follicules starts to end; the follicles that have quit creating are alluded to as atretic follicles, and they serve no further job. This is the moment when the development of specific extra follicules begins to dial back or stop out and out. When stimulated by LH, the lethargic follicle changes into the corpus luteum and initiates the development of progesterone notwithstanding estrogen. This happens after the follicle has exploded. This procedure is critical to ensuring that the pregnancy continues to progress normally. The process is carried out throughout the whole of the pregnancy. The corpus luteum is the organ that is responsible for the synthesis of the hormones inhibit and relaxin, despite the fact that these hormones are generated in considerably lesser quantities.

- **Fallopian tubes**: These thin tubes serve as pathways for your egg (ovum) to travel from your ovaries to your uterus. They are joined to the top part of your uterus. Your ovaries are answerable for creating eggs, and your uterus is liable for getting them. The fallopian tubes are the average location for the cycle that outcomes in the fertilization of an egg by sperm. In the wake of being treated, the egg will go to the uterus, where it will implant itself into the coating of the uterus. Inside a lady's regenerative system, the uterus is associated with the ovaries by a couple of cylinders known as the fallopian tubes. At the point when an ovum has accomplished its maximum capacity, the follicle that encompasses it as well as the mass of the ovary will break, which will permit the ovum to go from the ovary to the fallopian cylinder and start the course of fertilization. Whenever it arrives at that point, the developments of cilia that are situated on the internal covering of the cylinders drive it into the uterus. Cilia are tracked down within surface of the cylinders. This outing could require a few hours or conceivably numerous days to finish. On the off chance that the ovum is treated while it is still in the fallopian tube, it will regularly embed in the endometrium of the uterus after it arrives at the uterus. This is the principal sign that a pregnancy has begun. On the off chance that the ovum isn't prepared while it is still in the fallopian tube, it won't embed.

The uterus and ovaries are connected by two long, thin cylinders, one of which is the fallopian tube. After traveling through the fallopian tubes, eggs from the ovaries are delivered to the uterus. In the female reproductive system, one ovary and one fallopian tube are located on each side of the uterus. The lower region of the midsection is where these organs are situated.

Your fallopian tubes are an essential pathway that an egg, a sperm, and a fertilized egg (embryo) take in order to meet and for the fertilized egg to go to the uterus. This is how you become pregnant. Your fertility is directly influenced by the state of your fallopian tubes. Individuals and couples may have a more difficult time becoming pregnant if their fallopian tubes are damaged or blocked in any way.

The fallopian tubes are a couple of solid conduits that are empty and might be tracked down between the ovaries and the uterus in a lady's body. Every one of a lady's fallopian tubes capabilities as a path between her ovaries, the piece of her body that is liable for egg creation, and her uterus, the piece of her body that is liable for fetal improvement once an egg has been prepared. Because fertilization takes place in the fallopian tubes, this anatomical feature of your reproductive system is one of the most important contributors to your fertility.

A. *The role of fallopian tubes*

The fallopian tubes in your body are urgent to fertilization and pregnancy. Consider the fallopian tube as:

- **A holding place for your egg:** Every month, one of your ovaries produces a fully developed egg as part of your monthly cycle. The fingers-like fimbriae in your fallopian cylinder sweep the egg into the cylinder where it is held back to be processed.

- **The site where fertilization happens:** The sperm from your accomplice will pass through your cervix, uterus, and fallopian tubes assuming they ejaculate when you're in a sexual position. Your fallopian tubes ripen at the moment an egg and sperm come into touch.

B. An active passageway that moves a fertilized egg to your uterus

A treated egg (incipient organism) travels via your fallopian tubes and into your uterus, where it may develop into a child. In your fallopian tube, the developing creature is transported along places of significant strength.

C. Parts of a fallopian tube

There are four sections to a fallopian tube:

- **Infundibulum:** the section of your fallopian tube that resembles a pipe and is closest to your ovaries. It possesses fimbriae, which resemble fingers and extend in the direction of the ovary. The single fimbria known as the fimbria ovarica allows access to your ovary. The fimbriae capture an egg as it is discharged from your ovary and gently whisk it into your fallopian tube.
- **Ampulla:** between the isthmus and the infundibulum, the primary duct of the fallopian tube. The most typical locations for fertilization are ampullae.
- **Isthmus:** Your fallopian tube's intramural portion, which is the portion closest to your uterus, is connected to the ampulla via a small channel.
- **Intramural (interstitial) portion:** The portion of your fallopian tube that enters your uterus's top. It allows access to your uterus cavity, where an embryo may implant and grow into a fetus against your uterine wall.

1.4 HOW DOES REPRODUCTION WORK?

In humans, reproduction requires cooperation between the reproductive systems of the male and the female. Sperm and eggs are the two types of cells that are involved in sexual reproduction. It is possible for a sperm to fertilize an egg and produce a zygote when it comes into contact with an egg. This zygote will develop into a fetus in due time. In order for a human being to reproduce, they require both a sperm and an egg.

The female reproductive system enables a woman to:

- Produce eggs (ova)
- Have Sexual Intercourse
- Protect and nourish a fertilized egg until it is fully developed
- Give Birth

If a person did not possess the sexual organs known as gonads, it would be impossible for them to reproduce sexually. In common parlance, the gonads are synonymous with the testicles of a man. However, people of both sexes have gonads: Ovaries are the balls of females since they are answerable for the development of female gametes (eggs). The development of male gametes (sperm) happens in the balls of males.

At the point when a young lady is conceived, her ovaries contain countless eggs, which are all torpid until she arrives at pubescence. Adolescence denotes the start of her conceptive years. The pituitary organ, which is located in the mind, starts delivering chemicals with the beginning of pubescence. These chemicals drive the ovaries to deliver female sexual chemicals, including estrogen. Due to the outflow of these chemicals, a young lady will ultimately develop into a physically mature lady. As females approach the finish of youth, they begin to deliver eggs as a feature of a month to month time span that is named the period. This cycle is repeated consistently. During ovulation, which happens once a month by and large, an egg is set free from an ovary into one of the fallopian tubes.

Without fertilization by a sperm while the egg is still in the fallopian tube, the egg is ousted from the body something like fourteen days later by means of the uterus; this cycle is known as menstruation. The month to month stream, which normally endures somewhere in the range of three and five days and is made out of blood and the tissues that make up the inward coating of the uterus, is something that most females experience. The start of a lady's monthly cycle is alluded to as the menarche (MEH-nar-kee).

In the days paving the way to their periods, it is entirely expected for ladies and young ladies to encounter some degree of agony. The expression "premenstrual condition" (PMS) alludes to an assortment of mental and actual side effects that are capable by numerous young ladies and ladies in the days paving the way to their periods. A portion of these side effects incorporate the accompanying:

- Acne
- Backaches
- Bloating
- Constipation
- Depression
- Diarrhea
- Food Cravings
- Headaches
- Irritability
- Sore Breasts
- Tiredness
- Trouble Concentrating or Handling Stress

The symptoms of premenstrual syndrome (PMS) tend to worsen in the week leading up to a woman's menstruation and go away once her period starts.

Prostaglandins are substances produced by the body that cause the smooth muscle in the uterus to contract, which results in many young women experiencing cramping in the abdominal region during the first few days of their periods. These involuntary contractions might be mild or severe, depending on how acute or forceful they are.

It may take a girl's body up to two years after menarche to acquire a regular menstrual cycle after the onset of menstruation. During that period, her body is adapting to the changes in hormone levels that come with entering puberty. There is a wide variety of possible lengths for a woman's monthly cycle, ranging from 23 to 35 days, although the average length is 28 days.

- **Vaginitis**

Inflammation of the vagina, also known as vaginitis, is most often brought on by an infection. The gynecological affliction is seen the most frequently in patients. Since vaginitis might be brought about by a wide assortment of ages, various sorts of sexual action, and various strategies for microbial identification, pinpointing a solitary creature as the essential culprit is troublesome. There are different irresistible living beings that might cause vaginitis. These irresistible specialists exploit the nearby contact to mucosal layers and emissions. Vaginitis might possibly be brought about by a physically communicated sickness. The presence of vaginal release, which could have a specific tone, scent, or character, is many times utilized as the essential symptomatic figure instances of vaginitis.

- **Bacterial vaginosis**

This is an infection that may be seen in women's vaginal areas. In contrast to vaginitis, this condition does not include inflammation of the vaginal canal. Bacterial vaginosis is a polymicrobial contamination, implying that it is brought about by a combination of a few sorts of microorganisms. To affirm a finding of bacterial vaginosis, it is important to notice three out of the accompanying four side effects: There is a homogenous release that is extremely meager, the vagina has a pH of 4.5, there are epithelial cells in the vagina that have microorganisms sticking to them, or there is a smell that is off-putting. It has been connected to an expanded gamble of different diseases that might happen in the genital plot, including endometritis.

- **Yeast infection**

As per the Places for Infectious prevention and Anticipation, at least 75% of grown-up ladies have had vaginal irritation at least once all through their lives. This is a common reason for vaginal irritation. Candida abundance in the vagina might prompt yeast diseases. Candida is the logical name for the growth. Yeast contaminations are in many cases welcomed on by an acidic vaginal climate, which might prompt a pH unevenness and the ensuing development of yeast. Different factors, including as pregnancy, diabetes, a more fragile safe system, tight-fitting garments, or douching, may likewise assume a part in the improvement of this condition. Yeast diseases might cause various awkward side effects, including tingling, copying, irritation, and a release from the vagina that looks like curds. It has been guaranteed that ladies likewise persevere through difficult urination and sexual action because of this condition. A yeast contamination might be analyzed by gathering an example of the vaginal emissions, putting them under a magnifying lens, and searching for indications of yeast in the example. Creams that might be applied in or around the vaginal locale or medications that can be taken by mouth to stop the advancement of growth are both suitable treatment choices.

- **Genital mutilation**

Mutilating female genitalia is a widespread behavior that may be seen in many different cultures. The clitoridectomy, which is the circumcision of the clitoris, and the extraction of the prepuce, which is the skin that encompasses the clitoris, are the two types of genital mutilation that are played out the most frequently. All of these conditions have the potential to cause a wide variety of undesirable health effects, including bleeding, permanent damage to tissue, and sepsis, which sometimes results in death.

- **Genital surgery**

The term "genitoplasty" refers to the surgical procedure that is performed to repair damaged genital organs, most often as a result of cancer and the treatment for it. There are other cosmetic surgeries that may be chosen to alter the look of the external genitalia.

- **Birth control**

Women have access to a diverse range of methods for preventing unwanted pregnancies. Both hormonal and physical methods of birth control are available. Oral contraceptives may be helpful in the treatment and management of a variety of medical disorders, including menorrhagia. Oral contraceptives, on the other hand, have been linked to a number of adverse effects, including depression.

- **A note from Cleveland Clinic**

Sexual activity, fertility, menstruation, and reproduction are all processes that are controlled by the female reproductive organs. The reproductive organs of each individual have a somewhat unique appearance. It is possible for some persons to be born without reproductive organs or with organs of an abnormal form. Because of this, the activities of your reproductive system may be affected, which may result in painful sex, irregular bleeding, or problems conceiving a child. Get in touch with your healthcare professional if you are experiencing symptoms that worry you or if you have worries about your genitals.

CHAPTER - 2

Structure of Female Reproductive System

2.1 INTRODUCTION

Women are the ones who are responsible for bringing new life into the world, which is why the female reproductive system was developed and continues to play an important role. It is only fitting that we are familiar with the main component and auxiliary components of this display as this system enacts a supernatural event from the beginning of life to the birth of the forming life inside. from the beginning of life till the birth of the internal life that is forming.

The female reproductive system is structured in a way that allows it to fulfill a variety of activities. It does this by producing egg cells, also known as ova, which are necessary for reproduction. The eggs will be transported to the area where they will be fertilized by the system that has been created. The Fallopian tubes are the location of the egg fertilization process, which also involves the sperm. The following stage for prepared eggs is for the incipient organism to attach itself to the uterine wall and start the cycle that prompts a full-term pregnancy. The female conceptive system is also responsible for producing female sexual hormones, which are crucial for the continuation of the regenerative cycle, in addition to the roles already mentioned.

Ovaries, oviducts, vagina, cervix, uterus, and the outside genitalia are all important for the female regenerative system, which is situated in the pelvic region. The female conceptive system likewise incorporates the outer genitalia. The process of ovulation, fertilization, delivery, and eventually the care of the kid are all supported by these components, in addition to a pair of mammary glands that are integrated both physically and functionally.

The female conceptive system is inherent a way that permits it to play out various jobs. It is liable for the formation of female egg cells, otherwise called ova or oocytes, which are fundamental for proliferation. The eggs will be shipped to the location where they will be treated utilizing this method. The fallopian tubes are the common location where origination happens. Origination alludes to the cycle by which an egg is prepared by a sperm. After fertilization, the egg will continue to attach itself to the covering of the uterus, which will stamp the start of the principal phases of pregnancy. In the event that fertilization or perhaps implantation doesn't take place, the system is designed to menstruate (the monthly loss of the uterine coating). The production of female sex hormones, which are essential for the continuation of the conceptive cycle, is also the responsibility of the female regenerative system.

The term "reproductive system" refers to the collection of organs in the body that are responsible for the creation of children.

To have the option to survey the wellbeing of these systems, to advance regenerative system wellbeing, to really focus on conditions that could influence the conceptive organs, and to give client education concerning the regenerative system, medical caretakers need to have an exhaustive comprehension of the anatomy and physiology of the male and female conceptive systems.

2.2 INTERNAL STRUCTURES

2.2.1 Ovaries

- Ovaries are the ultimate life-maker for females since they produce eggs.
- According to its dimensions, it is around 4 millimeters in length, 2 millimeters in breadth, and 1.5 millimeters in thickness. It seems like it was made in the form of an almond. It has the appearance of being pitted, like a raisin, but its hue is more of a grayish white.
- It may be found in close proximity to the uterus on both the left and right side of the lower abdomen.

- Egg cells, also known as ova, are produced, matured, and expelled by the ovaries as part of their function.
- The ovary's function is to carry out these processes, which include the creation and maintenance of secondary sex characteristics in females.
- In addition to this, it is divided into three sections: the epithelium, which serves as a protective layer; the cortex; and the core medulla.
- The ovaries are the female balls, and they are the organs that are answerable for gametogenesis as well as the creation of sexual chemicals. Follicular improvement happens in the external cortex of every ovary, though the internal medulla of every ovary incorporates veins and connective tissue.

2.2.2 Fallopian Tubes

Each of the two fallopian tubes (sometimes referred to as uterine tubes or oviducts) is around 10 centimeters (four inches) in length. The ovary is contained inside the lateral end of a fallopian tube, whereas the fallopian tube's medial end exits into the uterus. Fimbriae are periphery like projections that are located at the finish of the cylinder that encases the ovary. These fimbriae generate flows in the liquid that encompasses the ovary, which thus bring the ovum into the fallopian tube.

The anatomy of the fallopian tube guarantees that the ovum will keep on pushing toward the uterus regardless of whether it can't continue all alone, as opposed to sperm, which are fit for voyaging autonomously. The layer of smooth muscle that lines the cylinder contracts in waves called peristaltic waves, which help with moving the ovum (or zygote, as you will find in a moment) down the cylinder. The covering, otherwise called the mucosa, is shaped of epithelial tissue that is ciliated and has significant collapsing. The development of the ovum toward the uterus is likewise facilitated by the general action of the cilia.

The fallopian tube is often where fertilization takes place. If an egg isn't prepared, it will expire within 24 to 48 hours and then disintegrate, depending on where it is, either in the uterus or the fallopian tube. The transformation of the ovum into a zygote and delivery into the uterus takes around four to five days (for more details, see Box 20-4: In Vitro Fertilization).

Regardless of whether it can't embed in the uterus, the zygote will in any case keep on developing into an undeveloped organism. This sort of pregnancy is alluded to as an ectopic pregnancy, and the expression "ectopic" signifies "in a strange site." The incipient organism that is shaping can possibly being embedded anyplace inside the stomach cavity, including the ovary, the fallopian cylinder, or even elsewhere. Since these different spots are not particular to create a placenta or to stretch to help the developing of a child as the uterus is, an ectopic pregnancy frequently doesn't go extremely far or for extremely lengthy. It is normal for the mother to encounter draining as the reason for the unconstrained termination of an ectopic pregnancy. At times, medical procedure might be expected to keep away from the mother from dying as a result of circulatory shock. It is possible for an ectopic pregnancy to progress normally and result in a healthy child; when this occurs, it is a testament to the flexibility of the human body as well as the progress that has been made in the field of medical research.

- Egg cells make their way to the uterus through the fallopian tubes on their route to their destination.
- A smooth and empty cylinder is separated into four segments: the interstitial, which is 1 centimeters long; the isthmus, which is 2 centimeters long; the ampulla, which is 5 centimeters long; and the infundibular, which is 2 centimeters long and framed like a pipe.
- The ovum is moved into the fallopian tube by tiny hairs called fimbria, which are tracked down on the pipe.
- The mucous film inside the fallopian tube is followed by a layer of connective tissue, followed by a layer of muscle.
- The peristaltic movements, which are what propel the ovum forward continuously, are caused by the muscular layer.
- There is a path that origination could take since the distal ends of the fallopian tubes are open.
- The labia majora, labia minora, clitoris, vulvar vestibule, urethral meatus, and vaginal gap are all depicted on the vulva. The labia majora and labia minora merge in front of one another to form the mons pubis, which is the layer that sits on top of the pubic symphysis. The vulvar vestibule, which is located near the labia minora and contains the vulvar vestibule, contains both urethra and vaginal gaps. On either side of the vaginal entrance are the openings of Bartholin's organs.
- The vagina is an adjusted development that extends from the vulvar vestibule to the uterus' cervix and is made up of flexible fibromuscular

and connective tissue. The distal vagina contains the introitus. The back vagina connects the first vagina to the back bladder wall, while the premier vagina connects the back vagina to the front rectum.

- The female reproductive system, also known as the uterus, is made up of the cervix and corpus. The topmost area of the uterine corpus is called the fundus, and the area of the uterus closest to the cervix is called the isthmus in the lower uterine segment. The three unique layers that can be found inside the uterine wall are the endometrium, the myometrium, and the serosa. The endometrium, which covers the uterine pit, may alter in thickness and shape in response to hormone stimulation. The layer of the uterine wall that is in the middle and has the most thickness is called the myometrium. It is made up of filaments from smooth muscles. The uterine covering's serosa is its shallowest layer.

- The uterine cervix is a spherical structure that borders the vagina and uterine hole. It has the ability to conduct electricity between the two designs. The mediocre cervix emerges into the upper vagina at the cervical os. The ectocervix, the portion of the cervix that extends into the vaginal stream, is fixed with stratified squamous epithelium. The endocervix, which lines the interior of the cervical canal, is made primarily of columnar epithelium. The area between the ectocervix and endocervix is where the transformation zone is situated. The transition from columnar to squamous epithelium marks this zone. The area of the cervix most frequently affected by cervical dysplasia and hazardous transformation called the transformation zone.

- The oocytes should go from the uterine pit to the ovary through the fallopian tubes so they might prepare the uterine coating. Fimbria, which are finger-like extensions on each cylinder located closest to the ovary, aid in advancing the released oocyte farther into the cylinder. The ampulla, the portion of the cylinder containing the largest lumen, is formed when the fimbria transform into it. The ampulla transforms into the isthmus when the lumen becomes increasingly constricted and extends into the uterus. The cylinder finally transforms into the interstitial portion of the uterus after entering the organ. The oocyte emerges from this aperture and enters the depression of the uterus as it travels through the cylinder.

2.2.3 Uterus

- It is said that the uterus is an organ in the form of a pear that is hollow and muscular.
- It may be found in the lower pelvis, which is posterior to the bladder and anterior to the rectum. Its function is unknown.
- It is thought that the uterus measures 5 cm in breadth and anywhere from 5 to 7 cm in length. it is 2.5 cm deep at its broadest portion.
- Weight-wise, it comes in at around 60 grams for women who are not pregnant.
- It is the job of the uterus to take in the ovum that has been released from the fallopian tube, as well as to offer a location for implantation and sustenance.
- In addition to this, it offers protection to the developing fetus.
- It consists of the body, the isthmus, and the cervix as its three distinct parts.
- The body, which is located at the top of the uterus, makes up the majority of this organ. This is also the portion of the body that becomes larger to make room for the developing fetus.
- The link between the body and the cervix is just a thin strip of tissue called the isthmus. During a cesarean section, this is the piece that is removed from the body.
- The cervix is situated such that it is only partially above the vagina, while the remaining portion extends into the vagina. It has a cervical os on both the inside and the outside, which is the entrance that leads into the cervical canal.
- The cervix and the corpus make up the female reproductive organ known as the uterus. The fundus is the uppermost region of the uterine corpus, while the lower uterine segment, also known as the isthmus, is the portion of the uterus that is immediately close to the cervix. The three distinct layers found inside the uterine wall are the endometrium, the myometrium, and the serosa. The endometrium, which covers the uterine pit, may alter in thickness and shape in response to hormone stimulation. The layer of the uterine wall that is in the middle and has the most thickness is called the myometrium. It is made up of filaments from smooth muscles. The uterine coating's serosa is its thinnest layer.

- The vagina, the uterine depression, and the uterine cervix are all connected by a cylindrical structure called the uterine cervix. It can serve as a conduit between the two designs. The mediocre cervix emerges into the upper vagina at the cervical os. The ectocervix, a portion of the cervix that extends into the vaginal canal, is fixed with stratified squamous epithelium. The endocervix, which lines the interior of the cervical canal, is made primarily of columnar epithelium. The area between the ectocervix and endocervix is where the transformation zone is situated. The transition from columnar to squamous epithelium marks this zone. The area of the cervix most frequently affected by cervical dysplasia and potentially dangerous transformation called the transformation zone.

- The uterus looks like an altered pear and is around 3 crawls long, 2 creeps in width, and 1 inch top to bottom (7.5 centimeters by 5 centimeters by 2.5 centimeters). It is located in the pelvic pit over the pee bladder and between the two ovaries. Furthermore, the uterus is covered by the wide tendon. During pregnancy, the size of the uterus extends dramatically, it turns into the home of the placenta, which gives sustenance to the incipient organism and hatchling, and the uterus ultimately brings forth the youngster. Illustrates the a huge number and layers that make up the uterus The fundus is the top part that is located over the kickoff of the fallopian tubes, while the body is the immense center piece that is located beneath the fundus. The cervix is located at the foundation of the uterus and is portrayed by its little end. This end opens into the vagina.

- An overlay of the peritoneum makes up the serosa, otherwise called the epimetrium, which is the most shallow layer of the uterus. The smooth muscle layer is known as the myometrium. During pregnancy, the myometrium's phones grow to account for the extending embryo, and afterward they contract in preparation for work and conveyance at the finish of the pregnancy. The endometrium is the tissue that lines within the uterus, and it has two particular layers. The basilar layer is a permanent layer that is close to the myometrium. This layer is vascular; however, it is an extremely thin layer. During each menstrual cycle, the functional layer undergoes a cycle of regeneration and loss.

- The extension of veins, which is stimulated by estrogen and progesterone created by the ovaries, thickens the useful layer with the goal that it is more helpful for the improvement of an incipient organism. If fertilization doesn't occur, the useful layer will be shed during menstruation. During pregnancy, the endometrium changes into the placental segment of the placenta, giving the placenta its maternal qualities.

- The vagina is a solid cylinder that is around ten centimeters long and extends from the cervix to the vaginal entry in the perineum (pelvic floor). The vagina is about four inches long. It is located in front of the rectum and behind the urethra. In most people, the vaginal entrance is partly covered by a delicate membrane known as the hymen. This membrane is frequently broken when a person has their first sexual encounter or when they begin using tampons during their menstrual period. During sexual activity, the vagina acts as a conduit for the passage of menstrual blood, as a receptacle for sperm that has been transferred from the penis, and as a precursor to the birth canal after pregnancy has reached its conclusion. After adolescence, the vaginal mucosa is a stratified squamous epithelium, which is a kind of epithelium that is relatively resistant to infections. The vagina's natural bacteria, which are known as flora, produce an acidic pH, which in turn serves to prevent the formation of pathogens.

The uterus, often known as the womb, has the appearance of an upside-down pear. It is a glandular organ called the endometrium that lines the inside of the endometrium, which is a hollow, muscular organ with thick walls. During adulthood, the uterus measures 7.5 centimeters (three inches) in length, 5 centimeters (two inches) in breadth, and 2.5 centimeters (one inch) in thickness; but, during pregnancy, it may grow to be anywhere from four to five times its normal size. The cervix is the part that extends into the vagina and is located at the lower, narrower end. When compared to the body of the uterus, the cervix is characterized by a more rigid consistency due to its composition of fibrous connective tissue. Both of the fallopian tubes make their way into the uterus from different sides, quite close to the top. The portion of the uterus that is located above the openings of the tubes is referred to as the fundus, while the portion that is located below is called the body. The body becomes smaller as it gets closer to the cervix, and there is a barely noticeable outward constriction at the point when the body meets the cervix.

Instead of being perpendicular to the vagina, the uterus is often anteverted, or turned forward, so that it makes an angle that is roughly equivalent to a right angle with the vagina. Both the amount of distension in the urine bladder and the amount of distension in the rectum have an effect on the position of the uterus. During pregnancy, the uterus develops to a bigger size, which makes it rise higher into the stomach cavity. This carries the uterus into closer arrangement with the vagina. Otherwise called an anteflexed uterus, and uterus that isn't conveying a pregnancy will have a little forward curvature. Different organs in the pelvis, the strong floor or stomach of the pelvis, explicit stringy tendons, and folds of peritoneum all assistance to help and place the uterus so it stays in its legitimate location. There are two wide tendons that are twofold layered, and every one of these expansive tendons contains a fallopian tube along its without top line and a round tendon, which relates to the gubernaculum testis of the, in the middle of between its layers. These wide tendons are viewed as among the supporting tendons. What's more, the place of the uterus relies upon the respectability of two tendons known as the cardinal (Mackenrodt) tendons, which are located on each side of the cervix. When contrasted with the general size of the organ, the hole of the uterus is amazingly minimal in size. The cavity is by and large trapezoidal in shape, yet during pregnancy it becomes flatter and the front and back walls reach each other. The triangle's position is thrown off, with the base at the point where the two fallopian tube openings meet and the zenith at the point where the uterus and cervix meet. Between the uterus and the cervix is where the fallopian tubes are situated. The cervix's trench flattens out from front to rear, with the central section of the river having a little wider width than the other parts. It has two longitudinal edges that cross it, and slanted folds that move from each longitudinal edge in a pattern that resembles the parts of a tree. The cervical waterway measures 2.5 centimeters, or about 1 inch, in length. The outer os of the uterus is implied to be the point at which the cervical canal enters the vagina. The outside of the os is essentially nothing, almost spherical, and frequently discouraging. After the delivery of a child, the outside of the mouth will have lips surrounding it on the front and the back, giving it a more cutlike appearance. The cervical trench is lined by a mucous film made up of several organs that create a clear, basic biological fluid. Cervical body fluid is the name given to this biological fluid. The top portion of this coating experiences recurring alterations similar to, but less frequently stated than, those that take place in the uterus's body. Throughout the course of the month, these progressions take place. The cervix's mucous film typically has a profusion of nabothian pimples, which are incredibly tiny lesions. Cervical smears are taken from this region to identify any early changes that could be warning signs of danger.

There are three distinct layers of tissue that make up the uterus. On the outside of the organ is a layer of serous peritoneum, which is a membrane that secretes a fluid that is similar to blood but lacks the cells and the clotting ingredient fibrinogen. This layer only partly covers the organ. When viewed from the back, it also covers the portion of the cervix that extends over the vagina and the back vaginal wall before collapsing back to the rectum. When viewed from the front, it only covers the body of the cervix. It merely covers the cervix's body in the front. The peritoneal layers that extend from the side of the uterus to either side mass of the pelvis frame the two wide uterine tendons. These layers may be located close to the body's edge.

The myometrium, which is located in the centre of the organ, is a muscular layer of tissue that makes up the majority of the organ's mass. It has a highly rigid structure and is made up of tightly packed, smooth muscle fibers that are not striped. In addition, nerves, blood arteries, and lymphatic vessels are all present. The muscle may be broken down into about three layers, each of which has fibers that run in a distinct direction. The outermost fibers are laid out in a longitudinal orientation. The individuals that make up the intermediate layer are disorganized and run in all different directions; this layer has the greatest thickness. The longitudinal and circular arrangements of the innermost fibers characterize their structure.

The mucous film, otherwise called the endometrium, is the layer of tissue that is located most profound inside the uterus. It lines the uterine cavity up to the isthmus of the uterus, so, all in all it progresses forward to line the cervical waterway. This is where it becomes consistent with the covering of the cervix. Various uterine organs might be tracked down implanted in the cell structure, otherwise called the stroma, of the endometrium. These organs open into the uterine hole and are a piece of the endometrium. Moreover, there are a lot of lymphatic compartments and blood courses present. At each phase of a lady's regenerative life, the endometrium takes on an extremely particular look. These progressions might be rather dramatic. At the hour of adolescence, it begins to give indications of arriving at complete development, and from that point forward, it demonstrates huge changes with each pattern of menstruation. It goes through additional transformations before to, during, and after pregnancy, as well as during and after the menopause and in advanced age. Most of these movements are achieved by the activity of chemicals, with the ovarian capability going about as the expert regulator.

2.2.4 Vagina

The vagina, whose name comes from the Latin word for "sheath," is the trench that runs from the cervix (the external finish of the uterus) in the lesser pelvis right down to the vestibule between the labia minora. The term vagina in a real sense signifies "sheath." The hymen is liable for safeguarding the entry of the vagina. The vagina is located front to the rectum and butt-centric waterway and back to the bladder and urethra, separately. The length of its front wall is around 7.5 centimeters (three inches), though the length of its back wall is approximately 1.5 centimeters (0.6 inch) greater. Its walls have fallen. The vagina is calculated in a vertical and in reverse course at a point. When contrasted with the pivot of the uterus, the vaginal hub makes a point that is in excess of ninety degrees. This point changes a lot relying upon the state of the bladder, the rectum, and whether the individual is pregnant. In a solid lady, the cervix of the uterus projects into the vagina for a brief distance and is for the most part constrained facing the back mass of the vagina. Thus, the vagina has hollows or breaks in the back, on each side, and at the front of the cervix. These are alluded to as the back fornix (which is located at the rear of the cervix and is the greatest), the lateral fornices (which are located along the edges), and the foremost fornix (which is located at the front of the cervix). More information on the location of the uterus in regard to the vagina might be found in the segment dedicated to the uterus.

To generate the recto-uterine pocket, the peritoneum or one more film is collapsed back over the rectum and covered the upper piece of the back mass of the vagina. This creates the recto-uterine pocket. A mass of tissue called the perineal body sits between the lower segment of the back vaginal wall and the butt-centric trench. This mass of tissue is known as the perineal body.

The mucous film and the external smooth muscle layer of the vagina are connected to each other in a closeness. A longitudinal edge might be found in the mucous film's midline, which can be tracked down on either the foremost or the back wall. Various rugae, otherwise called folds, stretch from the edges to one or the other side. These edges are alluded to be the segments of the vagina. The wrinkles that are in the middle between the rugae are more obvious on the back wall, and they arrive at their pinnacle noticeable quality not long before to the conveyance of a kid. As opposed to the situation in numerous creatures, where significant exfoliation (the shedding of the surface cells) may happen, the layer goes through next to no change all through the period. The main change that happens is in how much glycogen that it contains, which is a mind boggling carbohydrate that looks like starch. The coating of the vagina contains no organs, and any bodily fluid that might be available was created by organs that are located in the cervical channel of the uterus. A more immature inward roundabout layer sits underneath the more evolved external longitudinal layer that makes up the smooth muscle coat. The bulbospongiosus muscle is a striped muscle that is connected to the perineal body. This muscle circles the most reduced locale of the vagina and safeguards it.

There is a vaginal supply route that originates from the inward iliac vein, notwithstanding vaginal branches that originate from the uterine, center rectal, and inner pudendal corridors, which are parts of the interior iliac conduit. These vessels are near the vagina and add to the blood supply to the vagina. The pudendal nerve, as well as the sub-par hypogastric and uterovaginal plexuses, are the wellsprings of the nerve supply that goes to the lower locale of the vagina.

2.3 EXTERNAL STRUCTURES

The vulva is one more name for the female outside genital parts, which involve the clitoris, labia majora and minora, and Bartholin's organs. The vulva is frequently alluded to as the genitalia. A minuscule piece of erectile tissue might be seen front to the kickoff of the urethra. This mass is known as the clitoris. It is simply ready to respond to sexual stimulation, so, all in all its vascular sinuses become loaded up with blood. The clitoris' just capability is that of a tangible organ. The mons pubis is a fatty cushion that sits on top of the pubic symphysis and is covered by skin as well as pubic hair. The labia majora (lateral) and labia minora (average), which are matched folds of skin, broaden posteriorly from the mons toward the back stomach wall. The vestibule is the locale between the labia minora and the labia majora that houses the doorways to the urethra and the vagina, separately. These gaps are covered by the labia, which additionally safeguards the mucous films inside from drying out.

Bartholin's organs are located inside the floor of the vestibule; their pipes open into the mucosa at the vaginal entry. These organs are additionally alluded to as vestibular organs. During sexual action, the liquid that is created by these organs lubricates the vagina and guarantees that the mucosa stays sodden.

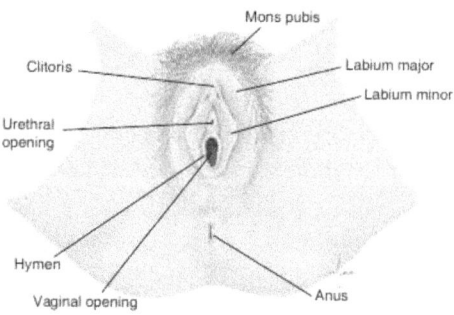

Figure 2.1: Female external genitals (vulva) shown in inferior view of the perineum

2.3.1 Mons Veneris

The mons pubis, regularly known as the pubic hill (at times referred to just as the mons, and referred to particularly in females as the mons Venus or mons veneris), is a circular mass of fatty tissue that is situated over the pubic symphysis of the pubic bones in human anatomy and in the anatomy of creatures overall. When seen from the front, the mons pubis makes up the forward portion of the vulva in females. It separates into the labia majora (signifying "bigger lips") on each side of the wrinkle known as the pudendal parted, which encompasses the labia minora, clitoris, urethra, vaginal entry, and different designs of the vulval vestibule. The labia minora are located on the contrary side of the pudendal parted.

Despite the fact that it's found in males and ladies the same, the mons pubis in ladies frequently has a greater perimeter. Because of the way that its fatty tissue is delicate to estrogen, a recognizable knock will seem when a female arrives at the period of pubescence. This causes the front part of the labia majora to be unstuck and created some distance from the pubic bone. The hill will likewise be covered with pubic hair eventually. It is normal for it to turn out to be less recognizable because of the decrease in how much estrogen delivered by the body that happens all through menopause.

- A cushion of fatty tissue that sits above the symphysis pubis is known as the mons veneris.
- The pubic hair, which are coarse and coiled, serve as a covering for it.
- It absorbs the impact and cushions the pubic bone.

When seen from the front, the mons pubis makes up the forward portion of the vulva in females. It separates into the labia majora (signifying "bigger lips") on each side of the wrinkle known as the pudendal parted, which encompasses the labia minora, clitoris, urethra, vaginal entry, and different designs of the vulval vestibule. The labia minora are located on the contrary side of the pudendal separated. Despite the fact that it's found in males and ladies the same, the mons pubis in ladies frequently has a greater outline. Because of the way that its fatty tissue is delicate to estrogen, an observable knock will seem when a female arrives at the time of pubescence. This causes the front part of the labia majora to be ousted and created some distance from the pubic bone. Furthermore, pubic hair will cover the hill as it creates. It is normal for it to turn out to be less perceptible because of the decrease in how much estrogen delivered by the body that happens all through menopause.

2.3.2 Labia Minora

- The labia minora are a pair of folds of pinkish-colored connective tissue that are stretched apart from one another.
- The mucous membrane makes up the internal surface, whereas skin makes up the surface of the organ on the outside.
- It is covered with glands that produce sebum all over the region.

2.3.3 Labia Majora

- The labia majora are located laterally to the labia minora and comprise of two folds of fatty tissue that are covered by free connective tissue and epithelium.
- Its purpose is to shield the external genitalia, distal urethra, and vagina from any damage that may be caused by an impact.
- It is blanketed with pubic hair, which acts as an added layer of defense against any hazardous microorganisms that may make their way into the structure.

2.3.4 Vestibule

- Inside the labia, there is a smooth, flattened surface that serves as the origin of the apertures that go to the urethra and the vagina.

2.3.5 Clitoris

- The clitoris is a little organ made up of erectile tissue that is round in shape and located in front of the labia minora.
- It is protected by what is known as the prepuce, which is a fold of skin.

- Because it is so sensitive to both touch and temperature, this is the area that serves as the nerve center for sexual pleasure and arousal in females.

2.3.6 Skene's Glands

- These glands, which are located laterally to the urethral meatus and contain ducts that enter into the urethra, are also referred to as the paraurethral glands.
- During sexual activity, the fluids produced by this gland act as a lubricant for the external genitalia.

2.3.7 Bartholin's Gland

The Bartholin's glands are two pea-sized complex alveolar glands that are placed somewhat posteriorly and to the left and right of the entrance of the vagina. They were named after Caspar Bartholin the Younger, who discovered them. Other names for these glands are larger vestibular glands and Bartholin glands. They produce mucus, which helps to keep the vaginal tract moist.

They are comparative in capability to the bulbourethral organs that are found in men. Notwithstanding, Bartholin's organs are found in females' shallow perineal pockets, while bulbourethral organs are found in men' profound perineal pockets. Both of these pockets are situated in the urethra. The length of their conduits is somewhere in the range of 1.5 and 2.0 centimeters, and they open into the navicular fossa. The conduits are associated two by two, and their openings might be tracked down outwardly of the vulva.

The Bartholin's organs are two pea-sized complex alveolar organs that are set somewhat posteriorly and to the left and right of the entry of the vagina. They were named after Caspar Bartholin the More youthful, who found them. Different names for these organs are bigger vestibular organs and Bartholin organs. They produce bodily fluid, which assists with keeping the vaginal parcel sodden. They are comparable in capability to the bulbourethral organs that are found in men. Notwithstanding, Bartholin's organs are found in females' shallow perineal pockets, while bulbourethral organs are found in men' profound perineal pockets. Both of these pockets are situated in the urethra. The length of their channels is somewhere in the range of 1.5 and 2.0 centimeters, and they open into the navicular fossa. The channels are associated two by two, and their openings might be tracked down outwardly of the vulva.

i. This is another gland in the body that is important for lubricating the external genitalia during sexual activity. It is also known as the bulbovaginal gland.

ii. It is equipped with ducts that go directly into the distal vagina.

iii. The secretions of both of these glands are alkaline, which assists the sperm in surviving in the vaginal environment.

2.3.8 Fourchette

There is a little lip on the bottom of the vagina called the fourchette. This lip is the female counterpart of the frenulum, which is the single most essential component of the penis. If the foreskin is still whole, it will adhere to the shaft at the y-shaped junction that connects the head to the shaft. This is the point where the head meets the shaft. It has a high concentration of nerve endings. In some women, it is really sensitive, and it is absolutely necessary to make the effort to locate it. If you have given birth before, this region may have been ripped or cut, which may lead to scarring and leaving the area sensitive and often uncomfortable. If you have given birth before, this area may have been scarred.

- This is an edge of tissue that is generated by the back converging of the labia minora and majora. It is located in the genital district.
- This is the tissue that is removed after an episiotomy in order to make the vaginal opening a larger size.

2.3.9 Perineal Body

Like other compartments in the body, the pelvic cavity contains an inlet and an outflow. The pelvic floor muscles (levator ani and coccygeus) block up the pelvic outflow for the most part. The perineal locale is the region of the body that is shallow (caudal in a standing individual) to these muscles and average to the thighs. A precious stone formed locale is best seen (with the patient's understanding) when the individual is in a lithotomy act, which is recumbent with the knees twisted, legs brought up in stirrups, and hips flexed and snatched.

The foremost and back apices of the perineum are located at the substandard part of the arcuate tendon and pubic symphysis, individually, and at the tip of the coccyx. The ischiopubic rami and ischial tuberosities on the two sides structure the anterolateral borders, though the sacrotuberous tendons structure as far as possible. The skin of the region is the perineal locale's outside limitation. It go on as thigh and lower stomach skin. The pelvic floor muscles and their covering sash cranially (inside) limit the perineum. An even line between each ischial tuberosity (interischial line) partitions the region into urogenital (foremost to the interischial line) and butt-centric triangles (back to the interischial line).

This article will examine the items in the perineum as well as anatomical contrasts between the genders. Neurovascular supply and lymphatic waste, as well as other remedially significant subjects, will be covered.

This is a muscle group that relaxes and stretches readily during labor and delivery.

- The majority of pregnancy exercises, including as squats and Kegels, are performed to strengthen the perineal body. This makes it possible for the body to expand more easily during birthing and reduces the risk of ripping the tissue.

2.3.10 Hymen

The hymen is a little piece of mucosal tissue that wraps around or partly covers the external vaginal entrance. It is also known as the hymenal ring. It is comparable in anatomy to the vagina and is a component of the vulva, which is another name for the external genitalia. Although the hymen may take on a variety of forms, a crescent-shaped look is quite typical in children. Other shapes are also conceivable. Estrogen is responsible for the changes in appearance and increased elasticity of the hymen that occur throughout puberty. The post-pubertal hymen may take on a variety of normal forms, ranging from thin and elastic to thick and somewhat hard, depending on the individual.Extremely seldom, it could even be totally missing. It is possible for the hymen to rupture or tear during the initial penetrative interaction, which often results in discomfort and, in rare cases, modest transient bleeding or spotting. There is a variety of information on the frequency of ripping or bleeding following the first sexual encounter. The presence or absence of the hymen as a sign of virginity is not a reliable indication. Despite the fact that "virginity testing" is still a widespread practice in certain cultures, surgical repair of the hymen is occasionally performed alongside the test in order to provide the impression of virginity. It is possible for hymen injuries of a lesser severity to heal on their own without the need for surgical intervention. from embryogenesis, which occurs from the third week of pregnancy and continues through the second trimester of pregnancy, the genital tract develops, and the hymen is produced after the vagina. The urorectal septum starts to create at week seven of pregnancy and parts the rectum from the urogenital sinus. At the finish of the 10th week, the Mullerian channels have moved far enough descending to arrive at the urogenital sinus, so, all in all they have framed the uterovaginal waterway and embedded themselves into the sinus. At the finish of the twelfth week, the Mullerian conduits combine to frame the unaleria, an early type of the uterovaginal waterway. At the finish of the fifth month, the vaginal canalization is done, and the fetal hymen is created from the proliferation of the sinovaginal bulbs. Here the Mullerian channels meet the urogenital sinus. The fetal hymen by and large perforates previously or not long after conveyance.

The innervation of the hymen is rather broad. In babies, the hymen is thick, light pink, and repetitive (folds in on itself and may jut). This is on the grounds that the newborn children are as yet dependent upon the hormonal effect of their moms. This effect is kept up with during the initial two to four years of an infant's life by chemicals that are created by the newborn child. Their hymenal gap is in many cases as an annulus (circumferential opening). Following the neonatal stage, the width of the hymenal gap (as estimated inside the hymenal ring) increments by around one millimeter for every extended time old enough past the neonatal stage. At the hour of pubescence, estrogen makes the hymen change into a construction that is extremely versatile and sinewy.

- This wraps over the vaginal hole and covers it.
- It is a resilient and elastic semicircle of tissue that is ripped during the first sexual encounter.
- This is a muscle that has a natural tendency to stretch during labor and delivery.
- Most of pregnancy works out, like Kegels and squats, are finished to reinforce the perineal body. This is finished to make it simpler for the perineum to grow during birthing and to forestall tearing of the tissue.

2.3.11 Mammary Glands

Mammary organs are associated with the skin because of their construction, however they are practically associated with the conceptive system because of the way that they produce milk to sustain kids. illustrates the anatomy of the mammary organs, which are located foremost to the pectoralis significant muscles and are contained inside the actual bosoms. A layer of fat tissue encompasses the glandular tissue on all sides. After pregnancy, the alveolar organs are liable for the development of milk, which then, at that point, goes down the lactiferous conduits to the areola. The pigmented locale of skin that encompasses the areola is alluded to as the areola. Milk creation is regulated by chemicals at each phase of the interaction

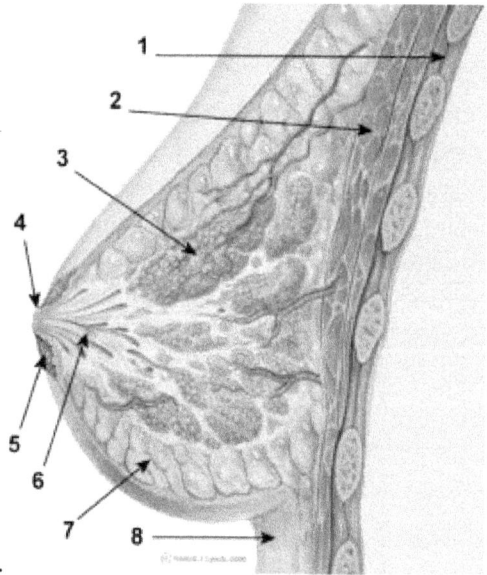

Figure 2.2: Mammary Glands

High measures of estrogen and progesterone all through pregnancy set up the organs for the development of milk once the child is conceived. After pregnancy, the real creation of milk is set off by a chemical called prolactin, which is discharged by the front pituitary organ. The demonstration of the infant sucking on the areola makes the nerve center get stimulated, which thus makes it communicate nerve driving forces to the back pituitary organ. This makes the organ produce oxytocin, which thusly causes the arrival of milk. Mammary organs are exocrine organs that are tracked down in people and different well evolved creatures. These organs are liable for the development of milk, which is utilized to feed infant creatures. The expression "bosom" in Latin is mamma, which is whence we determine "vertebrate." The mammary organs are coordinated into organs like the bosoms in primates (like people and chimps), the udder in ruminants (like cows, goats, sheep, and deer), and the dugs of different creatures (like canines and cats). These organs are answerable for the creation of milk. Lactorrhea, the irregular creation of milk by the organs, may happen in any warm blooded creature; nonetheless, lactation, the development of adequate milk for nursing, happens in many creatures just in phenotypic females who have conceived an offspring inside the most recent couple of months or years. Lactorrhea can occur in any well evolved creature. The hormonal guidance from sex steroids assumes a part toward its. There are a few mammalian species that are capable of breastfeeding in both sexes. Only under very precise conditions is it possible for men to breastfeed their children when they are humans.

Prototherians, metatherians, and eutherians are the three categories that are used to classify mammals. In the case of prototherians, both men and females have functioning mammary glands, however the mammary glands on prototherians lack nipples. Prototherians are classified as eutherians. These mammary glands are really sebaceous glands that have been manipulated. Only the females of metatherian and eutherian species have mammary glands that are fully functioning. Both "breasts" and "udders" are terms that may be used to refer to their mammary glands. In the case of the breasts, each individual mammary gland (for example, human mammary glands) has its very own nipple. In the case of udders, a single mass is made up of many pairs of mammary glands, and it has more than one nipple (also known as a teat) dangling from it. Sheep and goats, on the other hand, have just two teats projecting from their udders, in contrast to cows and buffalo, who each have one udder with a total of four teats. These sweat glands have been changed to become mammary glands.

CHAPTER – 3

Functions of Female Reproductive System

A few distinct jobs are performed by the female conceptive system. As well as empowering an individual to participate in sexual movement, it likewise aids the course of sexual generation in an individual.

Eggs are created by your ovaries. During the course of ovulation, these eggs are moved to the fallopian tube, which is the location where fertilization by a sperm might happen. After fertilization, the egg is moved to the uterus, where the covering of the uterus has become more vigorous because of the ordinary chemicals that are available all through the period (otherwise called the regenerative cycle). When the prepared egg has arrived at the uterus, it can possibly attach itself into the thicker uterine coating and create. If implantation doesn't occur, the uterine covering will be ousted as a period. Moreover, the female regenerative system is answerable for the development of sexual chemicals, which are liable for the upkeep of the month to month cycle.

The female reproductive system will eventually cease producing the female hormones that are required for the menstrual cycle to function properly when a woman reaches menopause. At this stage, the menstrual cycle may start to become erratic, and it may even end altogether. When a woman has gone a whole year without having a menstrual cycle, it is regarded that she has entered menopause.

3.1 MAIN FUNCTIONS OF THE VULVA

The production of progeny is the purpose of the reproductive system in females. In the case that the ovum does not undergo fertilization, it will ultimately go through the whole reproductive system, beginning in the fallopian tube and culminating in menstruation when it exits the vagina. Several transluminal medical treatments, including fertiloscopy, intrauterine insemination, and transluminal sterilization, may be performed on an individual via their reproductive system.

The exterior elements of the female reproductive system are collectively referred to as the vulva in medical terminology. In reality, the vulva is composed of a great deal of diverse structures, such as the:

- **Mons pubis:** On top of the pubic bones lies a hill of tissue known as the mons pubis. with a great many people, the pubic district is covered with hair.
- **Labia majora:** The folds of skin that are known as the labia majora might be tracked down underneath the mons pubis. They stretch out their inclusion to a few different region of the vulva too.
- **Labia minora:** These are the more inconspicuous folds of skin that cover the vestibule of the vulva.
- **Vestibule:** The space that may be found in between the labia minora is referred to as this. It is the passageway that leads to the vagina as well as the urethra.
- **Clitoris:** The clitoris, which might be found at the highest point of the labia minora, is an extremely delicate region that can be stimulated without any problem.
- **Bartholin's glands:** These are two minuscule organs that might be seen on each side of the entry of the vagina. They are situated in the genital lot.
- **Skene's glands:** These organs might be tracked down in the vagina, near where the urethra leaves the body. They could be a part of the Sweet spot and add to sexual stimulation somehow or another.

The main functions of the vulva are to:

Facilitating intercourse by going about as a wellspring of oil (Bartholin's organs) and padding (mons pubis)

Safeguarding the inner pieces of the female conceptive system (labia majora and minora

Assuming a part in sexual excitement and stimulation (clitoris); and safeguarding within segments of the female conceptive system (labia majora and minora)It safeguards the inside parts of the female conceptive system (labia majora and minora

Have an impact in sexual excitement and stimulation (clitoris)

Advance intercourse, for example, through providing grease (Bartholin's organs) and padding (mons pubis)

What's more, the female urethra may likewise be tracked down in the vulva locale of the body. This is the gap by means of which pee is released into the bladder.

3.2 MAIN FUNCTIONS OF THE VAGINA

The vestibule of the vulva serves as the location of the vaginal orifice that opens up into the vagina. This entry interfaces with the lower segment of the uterus, which is known as the cervix. The actual vagina is a strong cylinder that runs from this opening to the cervix.

It is possible for a small piece of tissue known as the hymen to partly conceal the entrance of the vagina. It is possible to rupture the hymen by sexual activity, the insertion of a tampon, or even through strenuous physical activity like riding a bike.

Now, let's take a look at the distinct roles that each of the components of the female reproductive system play in the body.

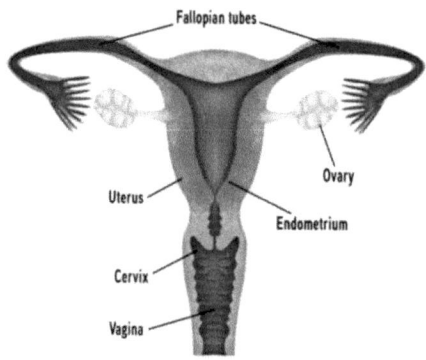

Figure 3.1: Functions of the Vagina

The main functions of the vulva are to:

- Facilitating intercourse by going about as a wellspring of grease (Bartholin's organs) and padding (mons pubis);
- Safeguarding the inward pieces of the female conceptive system (labia majora and minora);
- Assuming a part in sexual excitement and stimulation (clitoris);
- Safeguarding within bits of the female conceptive system (labia majora and minora).
- Receiving an erected penis or getting a toy during sexual activity.
- Acting as the passageway through which the baby passes during delivery.
- While a woman is having her period, letting her menstrual blood leave her body naturally.

Likewise, the female urethra may likewise be tracked down in the vulva area of the body. This is the opening by means of which pee is released into the bladder.

3.3 MAIN FUNCTIONS OF THE UTERUS

The fertilized egg is implanted into the uterus, which is the female reproductive organ. During pregnancy, the uterus provides support for the baby's growth.

- One of the main components of the female reproductive system is the uterus. It fulfils crucial roles throughout pregnancy and birthing.
- The term "endometrium" refers to the internal membrane that borders the uterus. Throughout the menstrual cycle, different hormone levels might affect this lining's thickness.
- For instance, the uterine lining thickens throughout a woman's cycle when her levels of the chemical's progesterone and estrogen rise. This aids in uterine preparation for receiving and caring for a fertilized egg throughout pregnancy.
- In the absence of fertilization, the egg starts to degrade. Progesterone and estrogen levels also fall. During your period, the endometrium and the egg leave the body.

- The egg inserts into the uterine covering and begins to create assuming that sperm prepares it. The uterus develops to products of its average size during pregnancy. The uterus is remembered to grow up to 1 centimeter (or 0.4 inches) consistently Confided in Source.
- The uterus contracts while the baby is being born. These contractions aid in the baby's birth by widening the cervix.

The uterus is a muscular organ that has the form of a pear and may be found in the pelvis of a woman. It may be broken down into two primary components, namely:

Cervix

- The lowest part of the uterus is referred to as the cervix. It is the structure that connects the vagina to the main body of the uterus.
- Location in the sow where the sperm are deposited.
- Sperm need to be moved from the cranial end of the cervix to the uterine lumen in order to fertilize an egg.
- Performs the function of a sperm reserve.
- Mucus is produced by the cow and the ewe, but to a much smaller level by the sow and the mare.
- Protected from the uterus by a "glue-like" material that is applied during pregnancy and serves as a barrier.
- During labor and delivery, it functions as the birth canal.

Corpus (body)

- This is the bigger and more important part of the uterus that is located here.

3.4 MAIN FUNCTIONS OF THE FALLOPIAN TUBES

The ovaries are connected to the uterus by the fallopian tubes. Each ovary has a corresponding fallopian tube that connects to it.

Eggs go from the ovaries to the uterus through the fallopian tubes during the process of becoming pregnant. Egg movement into the uterus is maintained in part by contractions of smooth muscles, as well as by the regular beating of microscopic structures that resemble hair and are termed cilia. The fallopian tube is a common location for fertilization to take place.

The fallopian cylinders' foremost job is to convey eggs from the ovary to the uterus. The fimbriae gather up the eggs and clear them towards the uterus. Peristalsis, or cadenced constrictions of the muscles of the cylinders, coordinates this development as well as the beating of the cilia. Fertilization ordinarily happens in the fallopian tubes. Sperm leave the uterus and continue by means of the cylinders, where they might come into contact with and prepare an egg.

The treated egg then, at that point, continues on its excursion to the uterus. An uterine pregnancy happens when a prepared egg inserts in the uterus and keeps on creating. To get pregnant without clinical help, eggs should be effectively moved through the fallopian tubes. To this end tubal sterilization, which keeps the cylinders from working, is a successful sort of long-lasting contraception. This is alluded viewed as having one's "reproductive ability limited." The uterine cylinders' essential job is to convey optional oocytes following ovulation. The fallopian or uterine cylinders are where fertilization happens. On the off chance that the egg isn't prepared, it degenerates here. Following fertilization, the zygote continues towards the uterus through ciliated epithelium and fallopian tube muscle activity The fallopian tube is where the incipient organism grows first. The incipient organism enters the uterine hole on the fifth day following fertilization and is embedded on the 6th day.

Following ovulation, the uterine tubes are responsible for the primary role of transporting secondary oocytes. The fallopian tubes and the uterine tubes both play a role in the process of fertilization. If the ovum does not get fertilized, then here is where it will deteriorate. Following fertilization, the zygote travels down the fallopian tube with the assistance of ciliated epithelium and the muscular action of the fallopian tube. This allows it to reach the uterus.

The fallopian tube is the site of the main phases of incipient organism improvement. After fertilization, the incipient organism advances into the uterine hole on the fifth day, and on the 6th day, it is effectively embedded.

The ovum makes a trip from the ovary to the uterus with the help of the uterine cylinders, which are liable for the essential capability of the uterine cylinders.

The accompanying models illustrate how the ultrastructure of the uterine cylinders assists with advancing the travel of the female gamete:

- Peg cells, also known as non-ciliated secretory cells, and ciliated columnar epithelial cells line the inner mucosa of the digestive tract. They guide the ovum toward the uterus and provide it nutrition as it makes its way there.
- The smooth muscle layer constricts to aid in the movement of the eggs and sperm down the passageway. Because muscle is hypersensitive to the effects of sex hormones, peristalsis is at its peak when oestrogen levels are up.

3.5 MAIN FUNCTIONS OF THE OVARIES

- The essential capability of the ovaries is to release eggs at customary spans. At the point when you are conceived, your ovaries as of now contain each of the eggs that you will at any point create over the span of for what seems like forever. Ovulation is the interaction by which a completely evolved egg is ousted from one of the ovary's cells one time per month.
- Additionally, ovaries are responsible for the production of a wide range of female sexual hormones. These hormones play a crucial role in the regulation of a woman's menstrual cycle as well as pregnancy. Progesterone and estrogen are two examples of these hormones.
- Ovaries fill three unique needs in the body. In the first place, they give a place of refuge and watchman the eggs that a female is brought into the world with until when they might be utilized. It is in many cases accepted that ladies are brought into the world with each of the eggs they could at any point require for their regenerative lives. In any case, research led by the School of Natural Sciences at the College of Edinburgh found that chemotherapy might stimulate the development of extra eggs.
- Both the monthly cycle and the method involved with becoming pregnant are subject to your ovaries. They are answerable for the creation of eggs, which are utilized in fertilization, as well as the chemicals estrogen and progesterone. Ovulation is the interaction through which an egg is let out of an ovary, and it happens about around the center of a lady's period (around day 14 of a 28-day cycle).
- There are many ovarian follicles viewed as on every one of your ovaries. Ovarian follicles are little sacs that are tracked down inside the ovaries and are answerable for the improvement of immature eggs.

The chemical known as follicle-stimulating chemical (FSH) is liable for the maturation of follicles in one of your ovaries once every month, between days six and 14 of a lady's feminine cycle. Ovulation happens when an egg is set free from the ovary, which occurs around day 14 of a lady's monthly cycle because of a sudden expansion in luteinizing chemical (LH).

- The egg begins its excursion to the uterus by moving by means of the fallopian tube, which is a design that is both slender and empty. How much progesterone develops as the egg goes down the fallopian tube, which helps with setting up the uterine coating for pregnancy. This happens in light of the fact that progesterone is created by the body.
- Ovulation is the cycle through which an egg that has been put away in the ovary for a later time frame is delivered.
- The ovary carries out the role of an endocrine organ and is liable for the development of chemicals that regulate the monthly cycle and pregnancy.
- The ovary is answerable for the creation of the egg as well as the discharge of chemicals related to female sexual movement.

3.6 THE ROLE OF THE UTERUS

The uterus is an important part of the female reproductive system and is one of its primary organs. During both pregnancy and labor and delivery, it is very crucial for a number of reasons. The endometrium is the name given to the membrane that coats the inside of the uterus. The amounts of the numerous hormones that are present during the menstrual cycle may cause this lining's thickness to change in a variety of ways.

Expansions in the levels of the chemicals estrogen and progesterone that happen all through the period of a lady, for example, lead the coating of the uterus to become thicker. This helps with setting up the uterus to acknowledge and really focus on a treated egg all through a pregnancy by setting it up. In the event that the egg isn't prepared, the course of its decay will start. Both estrogen and progesterone levels fall thus. During when you are having your period, the egg is removed from the body alongside the endometrium.

Assuming an egg is treated by sperm, it will insert itself into the covering of the uterus and start the course of improvement. The uterus grows to a size that is a few times greater than its run of the mill size during pregnancy. It's been anticipated that the size of the uterus might develop by up to 1-centimeter Believed Source each week, which is around 0.4 inches.

The uterus contracts as part of the birthing process. These contractions contribute to the cervix being more dilated, which in turn facilitates the birth of the baby.

The health and function of your reproductive system are directly influenced by your uterus. The following are the three primary functions of your uterus:

- During pregnancy, your uterus will extend so it can accommodate the developing child. It is likewise equipped for contracting to aid the removal of the child from the uterus.
- Richness: During the course of origination, a prepared egg will store itself in your uterus, and your child will foster there.
- The coating of your uterus is where blood and tissue are delivered during menstruation. This happens all through the feminine cycle.

CHAPTER - 4

Conditions Affecting the Female Reproductive Organs

4.1 INFECTIONS

Infections of the reproductive tract are referred to as reproductive tract infections (RTIs). The conceptive plot is a part of the regenerative system. Diseases of the conceptive plot might influence both the upper and lower regenerative lots in females. In females, these contaminations can influence the fallopian cylinders, ovary, and uterus. In men, these contaminations can influence the penis, gonads, urethra, or vas deferens. Endogenous infections, those that are caused by medical procedures, and the more prevalent sexually transmitted diseases make up the three categories of illnesses that may affect the reproductive system. Each condition is distinguished by its own unique set of symptoms and causes, which may be traced back to a bacterium, virus, fungus, or another creature. certain diseases are simple to treat and can be cured, while others are more challenging to treat, and certain illnesses, like AIDS and herpes, cannot be healed at all. An infection is caused by the invasion of pathogens into tissues, the subsequent proliferation of the pathogens, and the response of the tissues of the host to the infectious agent and the toxins that are produced by the pathogens. An infectious disease, also known as a transmissible disease or communicable disease, is a sickness that is caused by an infection. Other names for an infectious disease are communicable disease and transmissible disease.

Infections may be brought on by a broad variety of disease-causing agents, the most common of which are bacteria and viruses. The immune system of the host may be used to defend against illnesses. In response to infections, mammalian hosts first display an innate reaction, which often involves inflammation, and then they display an adaptive response. Antibiotics, antivirals, antifungals, antiprotozoals, and antihelminthics are some examples of specific drugs that are used in the treatment of infections. In 2013, infectious illnesses were responsible for the deaths of 9.2 million people, or around 17% of all fatalities. Infectious illnesses are the subject of study within the medical subspecialty that is known as infectious diseases.

The female reproductive organs are susceptible to a wide range of sexually transmitted diseases (STIs), including the following:

1. Chlamydia

Chlamydia, or all the more especially a contamination brought about by Chlamydia, is a bacterial physically communicated sickness that is brought about by the Chlamydia trachomatis bacterium. Most of tainted people show no side effects. The incubation time between being presented to the infection and having the option to taint others is viewed as some place in the scope of two to about a month and a half. At the point when side effects do emerge, they may not present for a long time after the contamination. Side effects that might be capable by ladies incorporate copying sensations during pee or vaginal release. In males, side effects might incorporate release from the penis, copying during urination, or uneasiness and expanding of one or the two gonads. Sporadically, the gonads may likewise amplify. It is workable for the contamination to stretch out to a lady's upper genital plot, bringing about pelvic inflammatory sickness. This condition might prompt fruitlessness or an ectopic pregnancy later on.

Chlamydia diseases might show themselves in locations other than the vaginal area, like the butt, the eyes, the throat, and the lymph hubs. Repeated contaminations of the eyes with chlamydia that don't seek treatment might prompt trachoma, which is a common reason for visual deficiency in pieces of the unfortunate world.

Chlamydia might be communicated by means of oral, butt-centric, or vaginal intercourse, and it additionally can possibly be given from a contaminated mother to her child during the conveyance cycle. In locations with inadequate tidiness, the illnesses of the eye may likewise be communicated through private contact, bugs, and towels that have been contaminated. It is an option exclusively for people to get tainted with the Chlamydia trachomatis microorganisms. Screening is the most widely recognized strategy for conclusion, and it is proposed that physically dynamic ladies younger than 25, as well as others who are at a greater gamble, and at the principal prenatal visit ought to go through screening. The cervix, vagina, or urethra might be cleaned, or the pee can be tried for the presence of the infection. Swabs taken from either the rectal or oral cavity are necessary in order to identify infections in those locations. It is possible to prevent the spread of the disease by either abstaining from sexual activity, using a condom, or engaging in sexual activity with only one other person who is not affected. Antibiotics, namely azithromycin or doxycycline, have been shown to be effective in treating chlamydia and curing the infection. In infants and women who are pregnant, erythromycin or azithromycin is the medication of choice. Partners in sexual activity should also be treated, and those who have the infection should be counseled to abstain from sexual activity for a period of one week or until they are symptom-free. Those who have been exposed to an infectious agent need to be tested for gonorrhea, syphilis, and HIV. After receiving therapy, patients should undergo testing one again three months later.

Chlamydia is one of the most predominant physically communicated illnesses on the planet, influencing around 4.2% of ladies and 2.7% of men. In 2015, there were more than 61 million new cases revealed all over the world. In 2014, around 1.4 million cases were kept in the US. Infections are most prevalent in those who are between the ages of 15 and 25, and women are more likely to get an infection than males. In 2015, infections were responsible for the deaths of around 200 people. The term chlamydia originates from the Greek word chlamys, which may be translated as "cloak."

2. Gonorrhea

Gonorrhea, at times spelled gonorrhea, is a physically sent disease (STI) that is brought about by the microbes Neisseria gonorrhoeae. It is more commonly referred to as the clap. The mouth, the vaginal region, or the rectum might all get infected. Discomfort or burning during urine, discharge from the penis, or testicular discomfort are all possible symptoms for infected males. Women who are infected may have pelvic discomfort, burning when they urinate, vaginal discharge, vaginal bleeding between periods, or vaginal hemorrhage between periods. As an example of a complication, pelvic inflammatory disease may occur in females, while inflammation of the epididymis can occur in males. However, a significant portion of persons who are sick do not exhibit any symptoms. Gonorrhea may spread to the joints and the heart valves if it is not treated.

Gonorrhea may be passed on via sexual contact with a person who has the disease. This encompasses both oral and anal as well as vaginal sexual activity. During delivery, the virus may potentially be passed from a mother to her kid. Testing the urine, the urethra in men, or the cervix in females is how the diagnosis is made. It is suggested that sexually active women under the age of 25 and those who have recently acquired new sexual partners undergo annual testing. The same guideline holds true for males who have sex with men (MSM).

The use of condoms, having sexual contact with just one person who is uninfected, and abstaining from sexual activity are all effective ways to avoid contracting gonorrhea. In most cases, treatment consists of administering ceftriaxone by injection and azithromycin orally. Due to the development of resistance to a large number of antibiotics that were previously used, sometimes greater dosages of ceftriaxone are necessary. After therapy has been completed, it is advisable to retest three months later. Additionally, sexual partners from within the last two months had to be addressed. About 0.8% of women and 0.6% of males are affected with gonorrhea in the United States. Out of the total 498 million new instances of treatable sexually transmitted infections (STI), which also includes chlamydia and trichomoniasis, there are an estimated 33 to 106 million new cases of gonorrhea per year. When a woman is a young adult is when she is most likely to get infected with a disease. In 2015, it was responsible for around 700 fatalities. (Leviticus 15:2-3) in the Hebrew Bible/Old Testament, there is evidence of writing that dates back to before the Common Era that describes the condition. Before the year 200 AD, the Greek physician Galen gave it its modern name. He described to it as "an unwanted discharge of semen" in his writings.

3. Herpes Simplex Virus (HSV)

Herpes simplex diseases 1 and 2 (HSV-1 and HSV-2), which are also known by their coherent names, Human alphaherpesvirus 1 and Human alphaherpesvirus 2, are two people from the human Herpesviridae family. This family is contained infections that are answerable for viral diseases in by far most of people. Both HSV-1 and HSV-2 are very far reaching and may effectively spread from one individual to another. They are infectious when a tainted individual begins to shed the infection into the climate. As of the year 2016, around 67% of the total populace under 50 years of age was contaminated with HSV-1. The pervasiveness of herpes simplex infection types 1 and 2 in the US is estimated to be around 47.8% and 11.9%, separately; notwithstanding, the genuine commonness might be far greater. It is one of the most predominant physically communicated diseases since it very well might be passed on by means of any sort of sexual or nonsexual individual contact.

4. HIV

The human immunodeficiency diseases, regularly known as HIV, are two special sorts of the lentivirus assortment, which is a subset of the retrovirus family. Helps (Helps) is a disorder that makes for a really long time and is portrayed by a sluggish breakdown of the insusceptible framework. This mistake makes it practical for perhaps lethal keen illnesses and malignancies to succeed. It is acknowledged that the typical proportion of time an individual could squeeze by following being polluted with HIV without seeking treatment goes from 9 to 11 years, dependent upon the HIV subtype.

HIV is a sickness that is truly sent in by a long shot the vast majority of models and may be acquired by contact with or the trading of blood, pre-discharge, semen, or vaginal emanations. Transmission of the disease from a sullied woman to her unborn youngster could happen in a manner other than sexual contact during pregnancy, during birthing through contact with the mother's blood or vaginal fluid, or utilizing chest milk. HIV is found in these body fluids as free disease particles as well as contamination that is contained inside safe cells that have been sullied. Research has illustrated (for both same-sex and other orientation couples) that HIV isn't transmittable during condomless sex if the HIV-positive accessory has a continually indistinct viral weight. This is substantial whether or not they are in that frame of mind with an individual of the other orientation.

Aide Lymphocytes, all the more particularly CD4+ Immune system microorganisms, macrophages, and dendritic cells are vulnerable to contamination by HIV. Dendritic cells are likewise defenseless to contamination by HIV. Disease with HIV causes low degrees of CD4+ Immune system microorganisms through various components. These parts consolidate the pyroptosis of vainly polluted Resistant framework microorganisms, the apoptosis of uninfected observer cells, the direct famous killing of sullied cells, and the killing of defiled CD4+ Lymphocytes by CD8+ cytotoxic lymphocytes that see corrupted cells. These parts add to low levels of CD4+ Safe framework microorganisms. Right when the amount of

CD4+ Lymphocytes falls under a particular edge, cell-intervened resistance is lost, and the body constantly ends up being all the more unprotected against canny defilements, which could incite the improvement of Makes a difference.

Human Papillomavirus (HPV)

An infection produced by a DNA virus belonging to the Papillomaviridae family is known as human papillomavirus infection (HPV infection). The majority of people who have HPV infections never have any symptoms, and 90 percent of them clear up on their own within two years. Moles or precancerous injuries might create assuming a HPV disease is permitted to remain and spread to different pieces of the body. Dependent upon the locale of the body that is assailed, these injuries could work on the likelihood of making harmful development of the cervix, vulva, vagina, penis, backside, mouth, tonsils, or throat. HPV is the causative expert in essentially all occasions of cervical dangerous development, with HPV16 and HPV18 addressing a large portion of cases. It is estimated that around 90% of HPV-positive oropharyngeal malignancies are brought about by HPV16. HPV is likewise associated with between 60% and the vast majority of different malignancies referenced previously. Both HPV6 and HPV11 are liable for countless instances of laryngeal papillomatosis and genital moles.

Human papillomavirus, a DNA infection that is an individual from the papillomavirus family, is the causative specialist of a HPV disease. More than 200 sorts have been portrayed. It is workable for a solitary individual to get tainted with more than one kind of HPV, and it is just realized that this sickness influences people. There are around forty distinct assortments that might be communicated by means of sexual contact and that can contaminate the butt and genital regions. Early time of first sex, incessant sexual accomplices, smoking, and low insusceptible capability are all hazard factors for ongoing contamination by physically communicated sicknesses. Other gamble factors incorporate an early time of first sexual experience. These assortments are fundamentally passed from one individual to another by delayed direct skin-to-skin contact, the most pervasive methods of transmission being vaginal and butt-centric intercourse. During pregnancy, a HPV disease may likewise be passed from a lady to her unborn kid. There is no proof that HPV might spread by means of regular merchandise, for example, latrine seats; by the by, the sorts of HPV that cause moles might spread through surfaces like floors. Since most hand sanitizers and sanitizers are not successful against HPV, there is a greater opportunity that the infection will be spread by inanimate irresistible specialists known as fomites.

Immunizations against HPV can safeguard against the most incessant sorts of disease. It is prompted that vaccinations happen between the ages of 9 and 13 years of age since they are best whenever given before to the start of an individual's contribution in sexual way of behaving. An evaluating for cervical disease, for example, the Papanicolaou test (otherwise called a "pap smear") or an investigation of the cervix following the application of acidic corrosive, may recognize both early malignant growth as well as strange cells that can possibly develop into disease. Screening makes it conceivable to start treatment sooner, which thusly prompts improved results. Screening has brought about a decrease in the complete number of cases of cervical malignant growth as well as the quantity of deaths brought about by the sickness. Freezing is a powerful treatment for eliminating genital moles. Sooner or later in their life, practically all physically dynamic individuals will get tainted with the human papillomavirus, frequently known as HPV. Around the world, the most common instance of physically communicated disease (STI) is brought about by HPV. There are around 570,000 ladies and 60,000 men who are determined to have a HPV-related disease every year. High-risk HPVs are the reason for approximately 5% of all malignancies that happen in the globe. Every year, around 36,000 individuals in the US are determined to have malignant growth because of having HPV. The World Wellbeing Organization (WHO) estimates that there will be 604,000 new cases of cervical malignant growth and 342,000 deaths brought about by the illness in the year 2020. Approximately nine of every ten of these recently analyzed cases and fatalities from cervical malignant growth occurred in nations with low or moderate salaries. Genital moles influence around one percent of physically dynamic people. Moles on the skin have been accounted for as soon as the time of old Greece, yet it was only after 1907 that specialists found that an infection was liable for their turn of events.

Syphilis

The microbes Treponema pallidum subspecies pallidum is liable for causing syphilis, which is an illness that is spread through sexual contact. There are four periods of syphilis: essential, optional, idle, and tertiary. The signs and side effects of syphilis change contingent upon anything stage the disease is in. Despite the fact that there might be a few wounds, the underlying stage is in many cases portrayed by the presence of a solitary chancre, which is characterized as a hard, easy, and itchless skin ulceration that is ordinarily somewhere in the range of 1 and 2 centimeters in width. A broad rash frequently shows up in patients who have optional syphilis. This rash most ordinarily influences the centers of the hands and the bottoms of the feet. There is likewise a chance of ulcers creating in the mouth or vagina. Dormant syphilis, which might wait for quite a long time, is described by the shortfall of signs or by not very many side effects. Tertiary syphilis is portrayed by the improvement of gummas (harmless developments that are delicate and noncancerous), neurological troubles, or heart grievances. Syphilis has been named "the incredible imitator" because of the way that it might incite side effects that are tantamount to those of a wide assortment of different sicknesses.

Sexual contact is the most pervasive gamble factor for communicating syphilis. Inherent syphilis may likewise be the outcome of the disease being passed from mother to youngster either during pregnancy or at the hour of conveyance. Sicknesses like yaws (T. pallidum subspecies pertenue), pinta (T. carateum), and nonvenereal endemic syphilis (T. pallidum subspecies endemicum) are additionally brought about by Treponema microscopic organisms. The three diseases recorded above are not normally spread by means of sexual contact. Blood tests are many times what are utilized to make a conclusion; in any case, microorganisms may likewise be found through the utilization of dim field microscopy. Testing is unequivocally energized for all pregnant ladies by the Habitats for Infectious prevention and Counteraction in the US. By wearing a plastic or polyurethane condom, one might eliminate the opportunities to physically send syphilis to their accomplice. Anti-toxins are a treatment choice that is very effective for syphilis. As a rule, an infusion of benzathine benzylpenicillin into a muscle is the best course of treatment for a contamination. Individuals who have areas of strength for a to penicillin could profit from treatment with doxycycline or antibiotic medication all things being equal. It is proposed to give intravenous benzylpenicillin or ceftriaxone to patients who have neurosyphilis. A reaction called as Jarisch-Herxheimer might show itself in patients getting treatment and manifest as fever, migraine, and solid irritation. In 2015, there were around 45,4 million people tainted with syphilis, of which 6 million were viewed as new cases. It was liable for around 107,000 fatalities in 2015, a critical reduction from the 202,000 passings it caused in 1990. In numerous nations, the disease rate has been on the ascent since the turn of the hundred years, and it frequently happens related to human immunodeficiency infection (HIV). Before the approach of penicillin during the 1940s, the contamination rate was considerably diminished, yet it has since developed. It is felt that this is expected to some degree to expanding sexual action, an expansion in the pace of prostitution, and a diminishing in the quantity of individuals utilizing condoms.

1. Trichomoniasis

It's possible that these illnesses won't cause any symptoms. On the other hand, in certain circumstances, symptoms such as swelling, discomfort, and abnormal vaginal discharge could be present. Injuries on the genital region might be brought about by various diseases, including HPV and HSV, among others. Complications from a few unique sexually transmitted diseases might go from gentle to hazardous. These may incorporate the improvement of threat, pelvic inflammatory illness (otherwise called PID), or the transmission of the contamination to a youngster when the mother is conceiving an offspring.

Trichomoniasis, often known as trich, is a sexually transmitted illness that is brought on by the parasite Trichomonas vaginalis. When infected, around seventy percent of those who are impacted do not display any symptoms. In most cases, the onset of symptoms occurs somewhere between 5- and 28-days following exposure. Symptoms may include itching in the genital region, a vaginal discharge that has a foul odor and is thin, burning while urinating, and discomfort when engaging in sexual activity. Having trichomoniasis raises a person's likelihood of contracting HIV or AIDS. In addition to this, it has the potential to create difficulties during pregnancy.

The most common routes of transmission for the sexually transmitted illness (STI) known as trichomoniasis are oral, vaginal, and anal sexual contact. The transmission of the disease may also occur via vaginal contact. People who are afflicted with the illness might transmit it even if they do not show any signs of having it. The diagnosis may be made by using a microscope to look for the parasite in the vaginal fluid, by cultivating the parasite in the vaginal fluid or urine, or by doing a DNA test on the parasite. If symptoms are present, then other STIs need to be tested for. Counteraction techniques incorporate swearing off sexual movement, utilizing security like condoms and diouching, and being tried for physically communicated diseases prior to participating in sexual action with another accomplice. Trichomoniasis is treatable with a number of medications, including metronidazole, tinidazole, and secnidazole, despite the fact that it is not caused by bacteria. Additionally, sexual partners need to be cared for. Within three months of therapy, around twenty percent of patients get infected once again.

In 2015, there were around 122 million newly diagnosed cases of trichomoniasis. Approximately 2 million women in the United States are afflicted with this condition. It is seen more often in females than in males. Alfred Donné was the one who originally discovered Trichomonas vaginalis in the year 1836. In 1916, it was determined for the first time that this sickness was caused by it.

It's possible that these illnesses won't cause any symptoms. On the other hand, in certain circumstances, symptoms such as swelling, discomfort, and abnormal vaginal discharge could be present. Lesions on the genital area may be caused by a variety of illnesses, including HPV and HSV, among others.

There are a few physically sent diseases that might cause possibly hazardous outcomes. These may incorporate the improvement of threat, pelvic inflammatory sickness (otherwise called PID), or the transmission of the contamination to a youngster when the mother is conceiving an offspring.

4.2 UTERINE FIBROIDS

When harmless (noncancerous) developments emerge on or in the uterus, this might prompt the advancement of uterine fibroids. The size of these developments could shift impressively. A woman could have recently a solitary fibroid or she can have a couple of fibroids all the while. Fibroids don't be ensured to achieve the presence of aftereffects. Exactly when they occur, you could get through things like troublesome pelvic fits, extravagant depleting during your period, and progressive pee. More often than not, fibroids don't address a prosperity risk. Anyway, there is conceivable that they could achieve issues like whiteness or pointlessness in unambiguous people.

Uterine leiomyomas, which are another name for uterine fibroids, are benign smooth muscle tumors of the uterus. Fibroids are another name for uterine fibroids. The majority of women who have fibroids do not have any symptoms, although others may have periods that are uncomfortable or heavy. If they are big enough, they may press on the bladder, which may result in an increased desire to pee often. They may also induce discomfort during sexual activity involving penetration as well as lower back pain. Uterine fibroids may range in number from one to numerous for a given woman. Even though it's not very frequent, there are certain cases in which a woman's fibroids might make it difficult to conceive a child. It is not entirely understood what causes uterine fibroids in women. Fibroids, on the other hand, tend to run in families and seem to be at least partially driven by hormone levels. Obesity and consuming a diet high in red meat are also risk factors. The diagnosis may be made by either a pelvic exam or with the use of medical imaging.

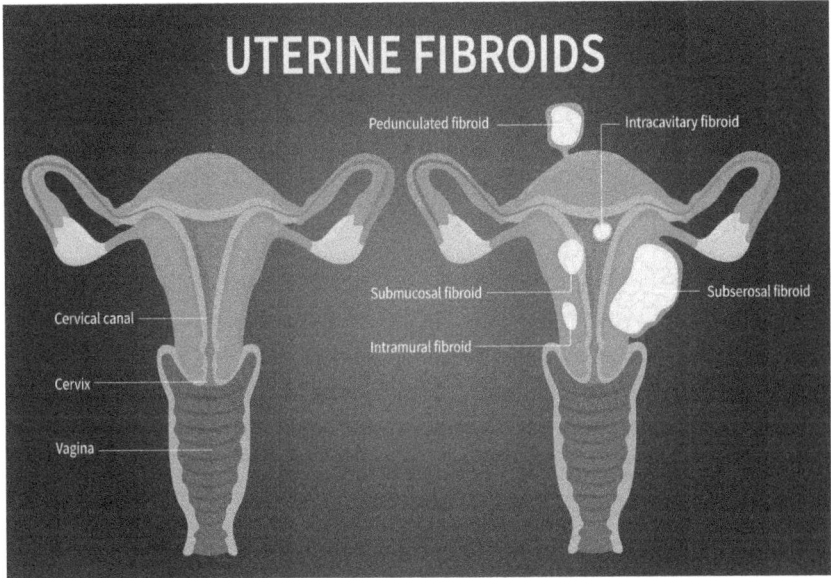

Figure 4.1: Uterine Fibroids

As a rule, treatment isn't needed on the off chance that there are no side effects present. Pain killers like paracetamol (acetaminophen) and nonsteroidal mitigating drugs (NSAIDs) like ibuprofen might help with agony and dying, individually. Iron enhancements could be fundamental for ladies who have extremely weighty periods. Although medications that belong to the family of gonadotropin-releasing hormone agonists have the potential to reduce the size of fibroids, these medications are also linked with a number of unwanted side effects.In cases when the symptoms are more severe, surgical removal of the uterus or the fibroids may be helpful. Uterine artery embolization is another potential treatment option. Leiomyosarcomas are very uncommon forms of cancer that manifest themselves in fibroid tumors. It does not seem that they originate from fibroids that are harmless. Between 20% and 80% of women will have developed fibroids by the time they reach the age of 50. It was projected that 171 million women throughout the globe were afflicted with this condition in 2013. They are more common throughout the reproductive years of the middle and latter stages of the animal. They often get smaller as a woman reaches menopause. Uterine fibroids are a frequent cause for women in the United States to choose for hysterectomy (the surgical removal of the uterus).

Fibroids are abnormal growths that may occur in the uterus. They are not cancerous since they are caused by an excess of normal uterine muscle tissue and because they are generated. Despite the fact that they are not cancerous growths, fibroids may cause symptoms depending on where in the body they are located. They are categorized based on where they are located. The symptoms and the therapy are different depending on where the fibroid is located. The accompanying graphic gives an explanation of its name and where it is located.

Medications prescribed for fibroids often work by affecting hormones in some way, such as by reducing the amount of estrogen that is produced in the body. They are often given for a period of three to six months and may reduce the size of fibroids by as much as fifty percent compared to their initial measurement. Sometimes the medications are administered in preparation for surgery in order to reduce the size of the tumor. The side effects of menopause, including hot blazes, vaginal dryness, upset rest, and changes in temperament, may happen as a symptom of this prescription. In the event that they are taken for over a year, there is a gamble that they might cause osteoporosis, frequently known as bone misfortune. Also, the utilization of different drugs is conceivable. Mifepristone, in some cases alluded to as a "next day contraceptive," can limit draining while likewise decreasing the size of fibroid growths. Danazole is another medicine, but it accompanies an extensive rundown of possible unfavorable impacts, including however not restricted to: weight gain, solid spasms, decreased bosom size, skin break out, hirsutism (improper hair development), sleek skin, temperament changes, sadness, lower HDL (or "great cholesterol"), and raised liver protein levels. Danazole isn't suggested for use in that frame of mind of any ailment. Oral contraceptives, when utilized in unobtrusive measurements, may assist with diminishing the unusual draining that is created by fibroids; however oral contraceptives don't treat the actual fibroids. It has been found that involving these drugs achieves a decrease in the probability of growing new fibroids.

A uterine fibroid is a benign tumor that forms in and around the uterus (womb). Fibroids are common in women. A myoma is another name for this condition. The muscular tissue of the uterus is where fibroids form in the female reproductive organ. It is also possible for them to develop in the fallopian tubes, the cervix, or the tissues that are close to the uterus. They might be so little that you cannot see them with the naked eye, or they can be as large as a melon. Their sizes can range anywhere in between. There is no limit to the number of fibroids that a person may have. The vast majority of fibroids do not need treatment.

There are a number of locations, both within and outside of your uterus, where fibroids have the potential to develop. Your therapy will depend heavily on the location of your fibroids as well as their size. The location of the growth of your fibroids, how large they are, and the number of fibroids you have will all play a role in determining the sort of therapy that will work best for you, if treatment is even required at all.

There are a couple names for the areas in and on the uterus where fibroids might be found when they are available. These names characterize the area of the fibroid, yet additionally the way things are connected to the encompassing tissue.

- **Submucosal fibroids**: There two or three names for the areas in and on the uterus where fibroids may be found when they are free. These names portray the region of the fibroid, yet also the status quo associated with the enveloping tissue.
- **Intramural fibroids**: These fibroids are actually a piece of the uterine wall itself and can't be eliminated. Think of the uterine walls as being similar to the walls of a home. Within this muscular wall, the fibroids continue to develop in size.
- **Subserosal fibroids**: These fibroids are connected personally to the outside mass of the uterus, notwithstanding the way that they are currently tracked down outwardly of the uterus.
- **Pedunculated fibroids**: These fibroids are also seen on the outside of the uterus and are the least prevalent form. On the other hand, pedunculated fibroids have a connection to the uterus in the form of a little stem. Because they begin with a stalk and subsequently branch out into a much broader top, they are sometimes compared to mushrooms.

4.3 ENDOMETRIOSIS

Endometriosis is a condition that happens when endometrial creates in region of the body other than the uterine coating. It is workable for this condition to influence the tissues on the outside of the uterus, the ovaries, the fallopian cylinders, or much other pelvic tissues. Torment in the pelvis is by a long shot the most ordinary sign of endometriosis. It's conceivable that this distress is progressing, or it could erupt during sexual action, during your period, or while you're utilizing the bathroom. The draining that in the middle between periods is another commonplace side effect.

Endometriosis has been linked to a decreased likelihood of achieving pregnancy. It is possible that other illnesses, such as some malignancies and autoimmune disorders, are connected to it as well.

Endometriosis

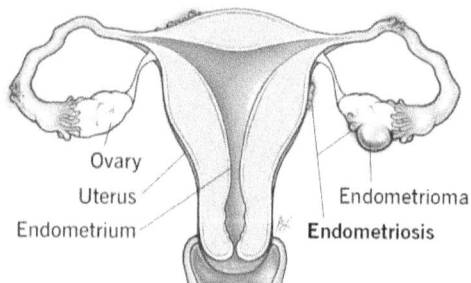

Figure 4.2: Endometriosis

Endometriosis is a problem of the female conceptive framework wherein cells that are like those found in the endometrium, the layer of tissue that commonly covers the coating of the uterus, foster beyond the uterus. This might cause various complexities, including fruitlessness and torment during monthly cycle. Ovaries, fallopian tubes, the tissue that encompasses the uterus and ovaries (peritoneum), the digestive organs, the bladder, and the stomach may all have sores, and the condition can likewise show itself in different segments of the body. Fruitlessness, pelvic uneasiness, weighty periods, torment related with defecations, agonizing pee, and pelvic agony during solid discharges are a portion of the side effects. Torment in the pelvis is capable by about portion of people who are beset, with feminine distress influencing the excess 70%. It is additionally very incessant to Experience torment during sexual movement. Up to half of the people who are burdened with the condition can't consider a kid. Around one fourth of individuals show no side effects, and around 85% of the people who are determined to have barrenness at tertiary focuses experience no uneasiness. Endometriosis might have repercussions in an individual's public activity as well as their emotional well-being.

The reason behind this is not completely understood. Having a history of the illness in one's own family is one of the risk factors. Endometriosis causes the regions affected to bleed every month (during the menstrual cycle), which leads to inflammation and scarring. Endometriosis may cause growths, although these growths are not cancerous. Symptoms, in conjunction with medical imaging, are often used to get at a diagnosis. However, a biopsy is the most accurate way to arrive at a diagnosis. Fibromyalgia, bad tempered entrail disorder, interstitial cystitis, and pelvic provocative illness are a portion of different circumstances that might deliver side effects that are very comparable. Endometriosis is a condition that is frequently misdiagnosed, and ladies oftentimes whine that they have been educated in blunder that their side effects are immaterial or run of the mill. There is a typical deferral of 6.7 years between the beginning of side effects and precisely procured biopsies, which are the highest quality level for recognizing the problem. Females who have endometriosis see a normal of seven specialists prior to getting an exact conclusion. Because of the time span it takes to analyze endometriosis by and large, it positions at the actual lower part of the analytic effectiveness scale.

The utilization of blend oral contraceptives is related with a lower rate of endometriosis, as per the fortuitous proof that has been accumulated. Practicing routinely and trying not to drink unreasonable amounts of liquor are other likely protection measures. Endometriosis is a condition that can't be relieved, yet there are different treatments that might assist with mitigating side effects. This might incorporate the utilization of torment medicine, hormonal treatment, or careful intercession. Naproxen is an illustration of a NSAID, which represents non-steroidal calming medication. This sort of drug is frequently recommended for the treatment of agony. Ceaselessly utilizing the hormonal part of oral contraceptives, for example, the conception prevention pill, or using an intrauterine gadget that contains progestogen may likewise be useful. Conceivable utilizing a gonadotropin-delivering chemical agonist, frequently known as a GnRH agonist, could assist barren individuals with having youngsters all the more without any problem. Endometriosis patients whose side effects are not very much overseen by elective treatment choices might be possibility for careful extraction of the sickness.

As of the year 2015, one estimate puts the number of persons impacted worldwide at 10.8 million. According to the findings of other researchers, the disease affects between 2 and 11 percent of asymptomatic women and between 6 and 10 percent of the overall female population. Moreover, magnetic resonance imaging (MRI) uncovers that eleven percent of ladies in everybody have endometriosis that has not been recognized however is apparent. Endometriosis frequently influences individuals in their thirties and forties; nonetheless, it might begin as soon as the age of eight in little kids. It leads to very few fatalities, with mortality rates of 0.1 and 0.0 per 100,000 people when age-adjusted and uncorrected, respectively. In the 1920s, it was discovered for the first time that endometriosis constituted a distinct disorder. Prior until that point, endometriosis and adenomyosis were treated as though they were the same condition. There is a lack of clarity on who initially characterized the ailment.

Endometriosis and the issues that go with it are among the most well-known purposes behind female fruitlessness. Endometriosis is a problem that is characterized by the relocation of endometrial tissue to places beyond the endometrium of the uterus. Side effects of endometriosis incorporate torment, fruitlessness, and unusual draining during period. Ovaries and fallopian tubes are the most regular destinations where stray tissue might be found, trailed by different organs in the lower stomach pit like the bladder and digestion tracts. As a rule, the endometrial tissue will connect itself to the outer layer of the organs, after which it will deliver grips, which are connections made of scar tissue and can tie close by organs together. Endometrial tissue and grips might block a fallopian tube, which keeps ovum and sperm cells from coming into contact with each other, or they can obstruct preparation, implantation, and, in exceptionally uncommon cases, the most common way of carrying the pregnancy to term in another manner. Endometriosis is thought to affect anywhere from one percent to five percent of women, with an associated risk of infertility ranging from thirty percent to fifty percent of this group. Endometriosis is often categorized from minor endometriosis all the way up to severe endometriosis using the updated method that was developed by the American Society for Reproductive Medicine. The severity of endometriosis is taken into consideration in both the treatment and management of infertility caused by the condition.

- Back pain during your period
- Severe menstrual cramps
- When you urinate or defecate, you experience pain, and this is particularly true during your period.
- Abnormal or excessive bleeding throughout the menstrual cycle
- There is blood in either your feces or your pee.
- Constipation or diarrhoea may be the result.
- An uncomfortable sexual experience Exhaustion that won't go away
- Trouble getting pregnant

4.4 POLYCYSTIC OVARY SYNDROME (PCOS)

PCOS is a problem wherein your ovaries are affected here and there. It is gotten on by a hormonal lopsidedness the conceptive framework. Subsequently, eggs might neglect to grow typically or might be kept from being let out of the ovary. Rare periods, skin inflammation, and expanded body weight are possible indications of polycystic ovary syndrome (PCOS). Fruitlessness, hardships during pregnancy, and the improvement of diabetes are among expected outcomes of polycystic ovary syndrome (PCOS).

PCOS, also known as polycystic ovarian syndrome, is the endocrine condition that affects reproductive-aged women at the highest rate. Cysts that grow on the ovaries of some persons with this ailment have given rise to the syndrome's name, despite the fact that this is not a uniform sign of the condition and is not the underlying cause of the sickness.

PCOS may cause women to have irregular or heavy menstrual cycles, excessive hair growth, acne, pelvic discomfort, problems conceiving children, and areas of skin that are thicker, darker, and velvetier. This condition is characterized by a number of basic symptoms, the most prominent of which are hyperandrogenism, anovulation, insulin resistance, and disturbance of neuroendocrine function. The prevalence of polycystic ovary syndrome (PCOS) has been reported to range anywhere from 4% to 18% among general populations. However, an assessment of the data from across the world indicated that the incidence of PCOS might be as high as 26% among some communities.

The specific etiology of polycystic ovary syndrome (PCOS) is not fully understood, and the therapy consists on the use of medicines to manage symptoms.

PCOS, otherwise called polycystic ovarian syndrome, is a problem where the ovaries make an unnecessary amount of androgens. Androgens are male sex chemicals that are regularly present in ladies, albeit in much lower focuses. The condition known as polycystic ovarian syndrome alludes to the improvement of a critical number of growths, or liquid filled sacs, inside the ovaries. Then again, a portion of the ones who have this condition don't have pimples, and a portion of the ones who don't have this sickness truly do have blisters.

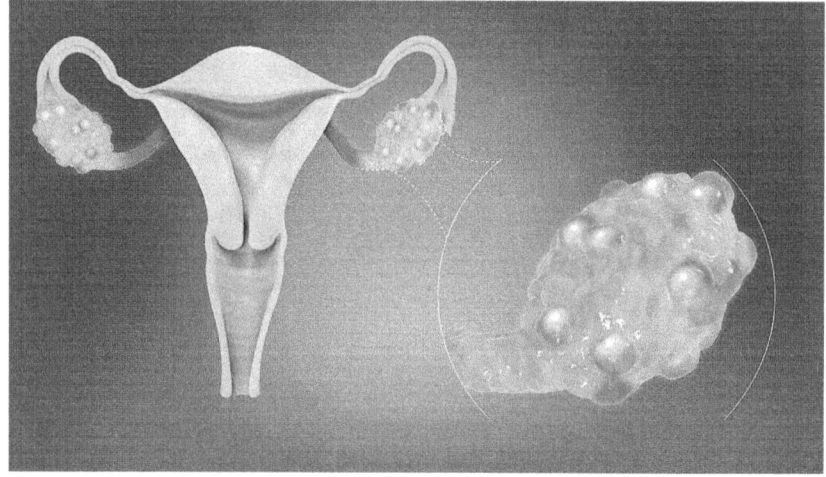

Figure 4.3: Polycystic ovary syndrome

Ovulation takes place whenever a fully developed egg is expelled from an ovary. This takes place so that it may be fertilized by the sperm of a man. If the egg is unable to get fertilized, it will be expelled from the body when you have your period.

In uncommon examples, a lady's body may not create an enough measure of the chemicals expected for ovulation. On the off chance that ovulation doesn't happen, the ovaries can possibly make various small sores. Androgens are the chemicals that are delivered by these blisters. Androgen levels are regularly raised in ladies who have polycystic ovary syndrome (PCOS). The period of a lady might turn out to be more hard to oversee thus. What's more, it's been connected to a few of the side effects of polycystic ovary syndrome (PCOS).

Prescription is often utilized as a feature of the treatment for PCOS. The condition known as polycystic ovary syndrome (PCOS) isn't treatable, albeit this limits side effects and forestalls specific wellbeing concerns.

At the point when a few ladies have their most memorable period, they might see the starting points of their side effects. Certain individuals don't figure out they have PCOS until after they've obtained a lot of weight or after they've attempted to get pregnant.

The most common PCOS symptoms are:

- **Irregular periods.** When ovulation does not occur, the uterine lining does not shed as it normally would each month. Some women who have PCOS have fewer than eight cycles per year, while others never receive their periods at all.
- **Heavy bleeding.** Because the uterine lining has more time to accumulate, your periods may be thicker than usual when they finally arrive. This is because the condition lasts longer.
- **Hair growth.** More than seventy percent of women who have this disorder develop hair on their faces as well as other parts of their bodies, including their backs, bellies, and chests. The condition known as hirsutism refers to excessive hair growth.
- **Acne.** A common side effect of male hormones is an increase in the skin's oil production, which may lead to breakouts on the face, chest, and upper back.
- **Weight gain.** Women who have PCOS have a much higher risk of becoming overweight or obese than other women.
- **Male pattern baldness.** The thickness of the hair on the scalp decreases, and some of it may fall off.
- **Darkening of the skin.** Crevasses of the body, such as those on the neck, in the groin, and beneath the breasts, are prone to the development of dark patches of skin.
- **Headaches.** Headaches are one of the symptoms that might be brought on by hormonal shifts.

4.5 OVARIAN CYSTS AND UTERINE POLYPS

Ovarian cysts are fluid-filled mounds that may grow on the ovaries. Ovarian cysts normally do not produce any symptoms until they burst or impede blood supply to the ovaries, in which case they can be quite painful. In the absence of therapy, they will normally disappear within a few months.

The inner lining of the uterus is a potential location for the development of lesions known as uterine polyps. These lesions are almost never malignant. They often do not create any symptoms; nonetheless, you may encounter the following:

- Irregular Bleeding
- Heavy Bleeding
- Postmenopausal Bleeding
- Prolapse, Where the Polyp Protrudes Out of the Uterus Through The Cervix

An ovarian cyst is a sac that develops internally inside the ovary and is filled with fluid. They seldom bring on any symptoms at all, which is to be expected. They are capable of causing symptoms such as bloating, discomfort in the lower abdomen, or pain in the lower back on rare occasions. The overwhelming majority of cysts do not result in any kind of harm. It is possible that the patient may experience agonizing pain as a consequence of either the rupture of the cyst or the twisting of the ovary that is caused by the cyst. Because of this, there is a chance that you may vomit up, that you will feel faint, and that you will perhaps have headaches. The majority of ovarian cysts are associated with the process of ovulation and may be classified as either follicular or corpus luteum cysts. Other forms of cysts include cystadenomas, dermoid cysts, and cysts that are caused by endometriosis. Polycystic ovarian syndrome, often known as PCOS, is characterized by the presence of several tiny cysts in both ovaries. Cysts are another possible complication of pelvic inflammatory illness. Ovarian cancer may sometimes manifest itself in the form of cysts. An inspection of the pelvis, together with further testing such as an ultrasound or other types of testing, is utilized to arrive at a diagnosis. Most of the time, cysts are discovered by simple observation over time. Medication such as paracetamol (acetaminophen) or ibuprofen may be used, if necessary, in the event that they are painful. Those who are regularly troubled by cysts may benefit from using hormonal birth control to stave against future occurrences of the condition. However, there is no evidence to recommend birth control as a therapy for the cysts that are now present. Surgery may be necessary to remove them if they do not disappear after a period of many months, if they get bigger, if they seem strange, or if they cause discomfort. The vast majority of reproductive-aged women have monthly outbreaks of tiny cysts. About eight percent of women may get large cysts before to menopause that will cause them trouble. After menopause, around 16 percent of women have ovarian cysts, which, if they are present, significantly increase the risk of cancer.

To begin, allow me to clarify the distinction between growths that form on cysts and those that appear on the cervix or the uterus. Cysts are the term used to describe growths that develop on the ovaries, whereas polyps are the term used to describe growths that develop on the cervix or the uterus. Cysts on the ovary are a condition that affects almost every woman, and although they don't always produce symptoms, there are instances when they do. Ovarian cysts do not often interfere with monthly menstruation; nevertheless, they may sometimes produce discomfort or pressure in the pelvic region. Ovarian cysts are most common in women between the ages of 30 and 50. On the other hand, each woman's experience with ovarian cysts is unique and different from the next. It is dependent on the woman's age, the size of the cyst, and whether or not there is a history of ovarian cysts in the woman's family.

Cysts may be divided into three categories: those that contain fluid; those that resemble a solid mass of tissue; and ovarian cysts, which can include both fluid and solid components. Each of these categories is essential, but the form of the cyst itself is also significant. For instance, small cysts that are filled with fluid and are perfectly normal are a part of the normal functioning of the ovary. A developing egg can also look like a small cyst, as can the corpus luteum that is left behind after ovulation. On the other hand, uterine or cervical polyps are overgrowths of tissue and are not normal.

The chance of developing cervical cancer from cervical polyps is far lower than one percent. The majority of the time, cervical polyps do not produce any symptoms; but, on occasion, they might cause bleeding in between periods. Cervical polyps can be found during a pelvic exam. They are only removed if they are huge (they may be as large as several inches), if there is an abnormal Pap smear, or if an HPV (human papillomavirus) test consistently shows a positive result.

The endometrium may also be referred to as the uterine polyp. It is characterized by an abnormal proliferation of the lining of the uterine cavity. Uterine polyps may either not produce any symptoms at all or can cause irregular bleeding in between periods. They can be identified by endometrial biopsy or through ultrasonography. It is strongly recommended that endometrial polyps be removed in order to address the abnormal bleeding, but removal of the polyps is also recommended because of the possibility of malignancy. Less than five percent of women between the ages of 25 and 45 who are diagnosed with endometrial polyps will go on to develop cancer as a result of the condition. Unfortunately, the danger rises with increasing age: endometrial polyps in women between the ages of 45 and 65 have a 9% probability of containing malignant cells, while in women beyond the age of 65, as much as 32% of endometrial polyps will be cancerous.

4.6 CANCERS

Cancer alludes to a classification of sicknesses portrayed by the development of unusual cells, which may either attack different locales of the body or spread across the body. Conversely, harmless growths don't metastasize to different pieces of the body. The presence of a bump, sporadic dying, an extended hack, unexplained weight reduction, and an adjustment of entrail movements are a portion of the possible indications and side effects. These side effects might be a sign of cancer, yet there are other possible clarifications for them also. North of 100 distinct types of cancer might happen in people.

The use of tobacco products is responsible for around 22 percent of all fatalities from cancer. Another 10% are attributable to being overweight, having an unhealthy diet, not getting enough exercise, or consuming too much alcohol. Other risk factors include the possibility of being exposed to ionizing radiation, certain infectious diseases, and environmental contaminants. [In the creating scene, diseases, for example, Helicobacter pylori, hepatitis B, hepatitis C, human papillomavirus disease, Epstein-Barr infection, and human immunodeficiency infection (HIV) are answerable for 15% of all instances of cancer. Different diseases that cause cancer incorporate human papillomavirus contamination and human immunodeficiency infection (HIV). In some measure to a limited extent, these substances apply their impact on cells by means of changing the qualities that they contain. Before cancer might frame, there are often various hereditary adjustments that need to happen. Cancers brought about by acquired hereditary anomalies represent around 5-10% of all cases. Cancer might be analyzed by the perception of specific signs and side effects or through the presentation of screening techniques. From that point forward, more demonstrative imaging studies and a biopsy are often performed to affirm the finding. By not smoking, keeping a solid weight, restricting liquor consumption, eating a lot of vegetables, natural products, and entire grains, eating safe starch, receiving an immunization shot against specific irresistible illnesses, restricting utilization of handled meat and red meat, and restricting openness to coordinate daylight, the gamble of fostering specific cancers can be decreased. Both cervical and colorectal cancers benefit from screening systems that consider early distinguishing proof. There is some discussion on whether bosom cancer screening truly gives any benefits. Radiation treatment, medical procedure, chemotherapy, and designated treatments are often utilized related to each other in the therapy of cancer. The treatment of agony and different side effects is a fundamental part of treatment. Patients who are at a high level phase of their infection benefit enormously from palliative consideration. The probability of endurance is corresponding to the sort of cancer as well as the phase of the sickness when treatment initially starts. In wealthy nations, the typical endurance rate following five years is 80% for kids younger than 15 at the hour of finding. In the US, the typical endurance rate for cancer over a time of five years for individuals of any age is 66%.

In 2015, around 90, 5 million individuals all over the globe were diagnosed with cancer. In 2019, there were an additional 23.6 million individuals diagnosed with cancer per year, and there were 10 million deaths caused by the disease throughout the globe. These numbers demonstrate increments of 26% and 21%, individually, over the first ten years. Cellular breakdown in the lungs, cancer of the prostate, colorectal cancer, and stomach cancer are the four types of cancer that influence men the most frequently. Bosom cancer, colorectal cancer, cellular breakdown in the lungs, and cervical cancer are the four types of cancer most frequently analyzed in females. On the off chance that skin cancers other than melanoma were remembered for the yearly all out of recently analyzed instances of cancer, it is assessed that skin cancer would represent around a little less than half of cases. In youngsters, the most pervasive sorts of cancer are intense lymphoblastic leukemia and mind growths, except for Africa, which has a higher rate of non-Hodgkin lymphoma. among 2012, there were around 165,000 analyses of cancer among kids younger than 15 in the US. The probability of creating cancer decisively ascends with propelling age, and industrialized countries have a lot higher frequency of many kinds of cancer. The rates are increasing on the grounds that more individuals are living to a mature age and due to changes in way of life that are happening in arising nations. Starting around 2010, it was anticipated that the yearly in general financial costs of cancer all through the globe added up to $1.16 trillion (US), which would be equivalent to $1.44 trillion of every 2021.

Cancer has the potential to impact practically every element of a woman's reproductive system, including but not limited to the following:

- Cervical cancer
- Fallopian tube cancer
- ovarian cancer
- Uterine cancer
- vaginal cancer
- vulvar cancer

It's possible for the symptoms of one kind of cancer to be very different from those of another. However, some indicators to watch out for include changes in the skin of the vulva, pelvic discomfort or pressure, and abnormal bleeding or discharge from the vulva.

Having a history of reproductive cancer in one's family, being infected with human papillomavirus (HPV), and smoking all contribute to an increased likelihood of developing reproductive cancer.

Finding, Therapy, and Treatment of Cancer that was distributed in June 2013. This issue has an assortment of top to bottom surveys that focus on the early identification and determination of cancer, designated treatment and therapy of cancer, chronotherapy, and the counteraction of cancer in difficult to-treat malignancies. Early diagnosis, identification, and treatment of cancer provide the best chance of successfully beating the disease. Self-examination and other screening measures are often able to detect obvious forms of malignancies such as melanoma and breast cancer prior to the advancement of the illness. On the other hand, there are a significant number of instances in which different forms of cancer are discovered and identified after the illness has already progressed and dangerous symptoms have emerged. A few incidences of cancer are discovered when a patient is being evaluated for or receiving treatment for another medical issue. Most of ordinary evaluating methodologies for cancer recognition are basically centered around the examination of cell morphology, tissue histology, and the estimation of organic liquids markers. Sadly, none of these techniques have adequate awareness or potentially particularity for the early analysis of cancer. In mark of truth, by far most of emitted proteins that have been researched as potential cancer screening biomarkers have either an unfortunate degree of responsiveness or a low degree of particularity. This may be because of the utilization of strategies that need responsiveness or it very well may be because of the way that a significant number of these growth markers are likewise created by cells or tissues that don't have cancer. Taken together, these perceptions loan assurance to the dispute that there is a prompt requirement for the advancement of new growth markers and innovative evaluating strategies to evaluate for cancer and controlling designated therapy. As of late, researchers and clinicians have moved their concentration to creative strategies to distinguish and portray biomarkers that drive the turn of events and movement of cancer, as well as to find upstream qualities/proteins that could be helpful to identify beginning phase cancer, anticipate guess, decide treatment viability, or to be novel medication targets. Likewise, distinguishing and portraying biomarkers that drive the turn of events and movement of cancer has permitted analysts to find upstream qualities/proteins that drive the turn of events and movement of cancer.

4.7 INFERTILITY

Infertility is the condition that occurs when a man or woman is unable to participate completely to the process of becoming pregnant, even after having an unsafe sexual encounter. It is possible to know what causes infertility or it may remain a mystery. In women, the most common cause of infertility is a fluctuation in their ovulation cycle. Infertility might have various causes, including however not restricted to low sperm creation, genetic issues, and other ailments. Infertility might be overwhelmed with the help of methods like in vitro fertilization (IVF), zygote intra-fallopian transfer (ZIFT), gamete intrafallopian transfer (GIFT), and other comparative techniques. The expression "assisted reproductive technology" (ART) alludes to a gathering of a few clinical control methods that are utilized to beat infertility. Embryo transfer (ET), in vitro fertilization (IVF), zygote intra-fallopian transfer (ZIFT), and gamete intra-fallopian transfer (GIFT) are a portion of the strategies that might be utilized. The overarching objective of these procedures is to raise the likelihood that a pregnancy will continue to term. Two of the disadvantages of antiretroviral therapy (ART) are the cost of treatment and how much time it takes.

Infertility is defined as the inability to consider a kid in the wake of trying for a time of one year. It is fundamental for remember that male and female factors could both assume a part in the event of infertility.

Infertility may be caused by any of the following conditions or behaviors in women:

- Factors that interfere with ovulation include polycystic ovary syndrome (PCOS) and Premature Ovarian Insufficiency (POI).
- fallopian tube damage caused by sexually transmitted infections (STIs) or scarring from a prior operation
- Endometrial conditions, such as fibroids or an improperly shaped uterus, might cause pregnancy complications.

A woman's chance of infertility might also be increased by a number of other circumstances. Some examples include becoming older, smoking, and being under a tremendous amount of mental or physical stress. The inability of a human, animal, or plant to reproduce as a result of natural processes is referred to as infertility. It is not often the natural condition of a healthy adult, with one notable exception: some eusocial species, the majority of which are insects that are haplodiploid. It is natural for a human kid or other young children to be in this condition since they have not yet reached puberty, the age at which the body begins to develop the ability for reproduction.

In humans, infertility is defined as the failure to achieve pregnancy after a period of one year during which a male and female partner have engaged in unprotected and consistent sexual activity. There are several factors that may lead to infertility, and some of these factors can be treated by medical intervention. Approximately five percent of all heterosexual couples in the globe are thought to have an unsolved issue with infertility, according to estimates from 1997. However, many more couples than that find themselves unable to voluntarily have children for a period of at least one year; estimates vary from 12% to 28% of all couples. Age is the primary factor responsible for male and female infertility in humans, and a mother's advanced age might increase the likelihood that she will have a spontaneous abortion while she is pregnant.

Male infertility is answerable for 20-30% of infertility cases, while female infertility accounts for 20-35% of infertility cases, and combined messes in both the male and female reproductive frameworks account for 25-40% of infertility cases. In 10-20% of the instances, the reason cannot be determined. Age is the leading supporter of female infertility, which often introduces itself as irregular or non-existent menstrual cycles in the affected woman. The quality of the semen is often utilized as a stand-in for measuring a man's ability to father youngsters. The most prevalent cause of male infertility is a deficiency in the semen. Fertile women have their most fertile phase just before and during ovulation, and then they are sterile for the remainder of their menstrual cycle, making them unable to have children. Tracking shifts in cervical mucus or basal body temperature are two examples of the fertility awareness tools that may be used to determine when these changes take place.

Infertility is defined as the inability to obtain a clinical pregnancy following a time of a year or a greater amount of regular, unprotected sexual intercourse. This is the medical definition of infertility. The World Health Organization (WHO) has recognized it as a problem that has to be addressed in the area of public health. It is regarded to be one of the most significant health issues that is not given enough attention, especially in developing nations. It is believed that there are between 60 and 80 million infertile couples in the globe, of whom between 25 and 28 percent (15–20 million) are located in India alone. Although the care of infertility is not a priority when it comes to public health in India, population control is, and despite this, infertility is a problem that is of utmost concern to the couples who struggle with it. If a woman is unable to conceive a child in a culture such as India, where being a woman is inextricably linked to becoming a mother, she may experience a great deal of emotional and social pain. This is in addition to the social and familial pressures that come along with the situation. It is possible to partition the reasons for a couple's inability to consider into four categories: (I) male factor; (ii) female factor; (iii) blended male and female factor; and (iv) unexplained factor. About a little less than half of instances of infertility may be attributed to female factors, 40% to male factors, and 20% to a blend of the two. Semen parameter abnormalities, varicoceles, congenital and acquired urogenital abnormalities, endocrine disturbances, genetic abnormalities, infections of the genital tract, obstacle in the reproductive canal, immunological factors, and openness to medications or toxins are a portion of the problems that may cause male infertility. The female partner has to have two things in place for a pregnancy to implantation take place effectively: a normal reproductive tract that is favorable to the transfer of spermatozoa and the release of an excellent egg when the endometrium is responsive for. Both of these things need to happen when the endometrium is ready for implantation. Infertility in ladies may be attributed to the interruption or asynchrony of any one of these events. Ovulatory pathologies, tubal/tubo-peritoneal pathologies, ovarian pathologies, uterine causes, endometriosis, endocrinological abnormalities, anatomical abnormalities, and cervical pathologies are just not many of the normal factors that may add to female factor infertility.

✓ Anovulatory infertility

Anovulation is an issue that affects a significant percentage of infertile couples. In order for ovulation to take place normally, there must be no disruptions in the hypothalamic-pituitary-ovarian (HPO) axis. Norm gonadotropic, hypogonadotropic, and hyperprolactinemic anovulation are the four types of anovulation that occur most often. As is the situation with PCOS women, abnormal levels of FSH and estradiol (E2) are seen in less than eighty percent of anovulatory individuals with WHO type II anovulation. In under a modest amount of the cases, the condition is caused by decreased degrees of the two gonadotropins and E2, which ultimately leads to pituitary failure (WHO type I anovulation). In the remaining 10% of ladies, chronically elevated FSH (>40 IU/L) and E2 levels (>80 pg/dl) are detected, which is predictable with premature ovarian failure (POF). This kind of anovulation is known as WHO type III anovulation. A pituitary adenoma, either mega or micro, as well as pituitary function problems, are the root cause of hyperprolactinemic anovulation.

✓ Polycystic ovarian syndrome

PCOS is the most common factor contributing to anovulatory infertility, which is also related with menstrual abnormalities, hyperandrogenism, and insulin resistance. PCOS is defined by the Rotterdam criteria (2004) as having any two of the following side effects once the associated conditions have been precluded: (I) oligo-or anovulation (ii) clinical and/or biochemical proof of hyperandrogenism (iii) polycystic ovaries. Along with the potential of an innate aberration in folliculogenesis, hyperandrogenism and hyperinsulinemia appear to have an impact on the advancement of anovulation in ladies who have PCOS.

✓ POF or early menopause

In ladies younger than 40 years, premature ovarian failure (POF) is the event of early menopause or hypergonadotropic hypoestrogenic amenorrhoea and early depletion of ovarian hold. Both of these side effects may be caused by POF. POF affects around 1 in 1000 ladies before the age of 30, 1 in 250 ladies by the age of 35, and 1 in 100 ladies by the age of 40. POF is idiopathic in the majority of cases (74-90%), but it may run in families (4-33%) or happen by chance. Despite the fact that the etiology of the ailment is often unclear, there are various factors that have been linked to it, including genetic abnormalities, autoimmune disease, iatrogenic following a medical procedure around the ovaries, cytotoxic medicines, smoking, radiation or chemotherapy, enzymatic and metabolic.

✓ *Luteinized unruptured follicle (LUF)*

LUF is a kind of anovulation that may cause infertility and is generally seen in around 10% of rich ladies and in 25% to 43% of ladies who are unable to have youngsters. Despite the ascent in LH, the ovulatory follicle doesn't break; nonetheless, the luteal phase isn't interrupted since the granulosa cells are luteinized with a normal amount of progesterone. Infertility that cannot be explained, endometriosis, pelvic adhesions, and the usage of prostaglandin inhibitors are a portion of the circumstances that have been linked to LUF. The actual etiology of LUF is obscure.

✓ *Luteal phase defect (LPD)*

It has been hypothesized that luteal dysfunction, also known as LPD, might be the root cause of infertility as well as the premature termination of pregnancies. The more seasoned thought of histological dating of the endometrium demonstrating maturation delay of over two days for the diagnosis of LPD is not generally utilized because of the prevalence of out-of-phase endometrium in ripe ladies. This is because of the fact that out-of-phase endometrium happens often in these ladies. Nowadays, a short luteal phase (under 13 days) and/or insufficient progesterone creation are expected to make a diagnosis of LPD.

CHAPTER - 5

Female Reproductive System Anatomy and Physiology

Anatomy and physiology are two branches of science that are firmly associated with each other. Because they are often canvassed in the same school classes, becoming confounded about the distinctions between the two is straightforward. To put it another way, anatomy is the investigation of the design and character of real parts, while physiology is the investigation of how these body parts operate and how they interface with each other. Morphology is a broad discipline, and anatomy is one of its subfields. Morphology is the investigation of an organism's internal and external appearance (like its shape, size, and pattern), as well as the structure and position of its outside and internal parts (like bones and organs - - anatomy). Morphology is a subfield of anatomy. An anatomist is a medical professional who specializes in anatomy. Anatomists gather data from both live and dead species, and the majority of the time, they use analyzation to learn about the internal anatomy of their subjects.

Macroscopic anatomy, sometimes known as gross anatomy, and microscopic anatomy are the two sub-disciplines that make up the field of anatomy. The study of gross anatomy concentrates on the human body in its whole, as well as the identification and description of bodily parts that are big enough to be seen by the human eye alone. The many forms of microscopy and histology are the tools that are used in the study of microscopic anatomy, which focuses on the architecture of individual cells. Because the structure and location of cells, tissues, and organs are directly connected to function, physiologists need to have a strong understanding of anatomy. When many subjects are covered in one semester, anatomy is often taught first. If the two subjects are taught independently, then anatomy could be required to take physiology. The examination of live specimens and tissues is essential for the field of physiology. In contrast to a physiology lab, an anatomy lab focuses largely on dissection to identify the response of cells or systems to change. However, a physiology lab may also incorporate other types of experiments. There are various subspecialties within the field of physiology. A physiologist's primary area of interest may be the reproductive system or the excretory system, for instance.

The investigation of anatomy and physiology remain inseparable with each other. A x-ray technician may find an atypical irregularity (a change in the body's gross anatomy), which could lead to a biopsy, in which the tissue would be inspected on a minuscule level for abnormalities (a change in the body's minute anatomy), or a test searching for a disease sign in the urine or blood (a change in the body's physiology).

5.1 FEMALE REPRODUCTIVE ANATOMY

Family planning counselling requires not just an understanding of the anatomy and physiology of reproductive systems but also a level of comfort in discussing these aspects of one's body. The components and roles of both the internal and exterior female anatomy, in addition to the physiological aspects of the menstrual cycle and the transition into and out of menopause.

The female reproductive system is structured in a way that allows it to fulfill a variety of activities. It does this by producing egg cells, also known as ova, which are necessary for reproduction. The eggs will be transported to the area where they will be fertilized by the system that has been created. The Fallopian tubes are the location of the egg fertilization process, which also involves the sperm. The next step for fertilized eggs is for the embryo to attach itself to the uterine wall and begin the process that leads to a full-term pregnancy. In addition to the tasks described above, the female reproductive system is also responsible for the generation of female sexual hormones, which are necessary for the continuation of the reproductive cycle.

Ovaries, oviducts, vagina, cervix, uterus, and the external genitalia are all part of the female reproductive framework, which is situated in the pelvic area. The female reproductive framework also includes the external genitalia. The course of ovulation, fertilization, conveyance, and eventually the care of the youngster are all upheld by these parts, in addition to a pair of mammary glands that are integrated both physically and functionally.

5.1.1 External Female Genitalia

The collective name for the exterior female reproductive structures is the vulva these structures may be seen below. A cushion of fat that sits directly on top of the pubic bone is known as the mons pubis. When a person reaches puberty, pubic hair begins to cover it. The labia majora (labia, and that means "lips" and majora, and that means "larger") are skin creases that originate immediately back to the mons pubis. Inside of the labia majora are the thinner and more pigmented labia minora (where labia mean "lips" and minora means "smaller"). Both the labia majora and minora effectively guard the female urethra as well as the opening to the reproductive framework in females.

The anterior areas of the labia minora meet up to encompass the clitoris, also known as the glans clitoris. The clitoris is an organ that creates from the same cells as the glans penis and has countless nerves, the two of which add to its significance in sexual pleasure and in orgasmic experience. A thin membrane known as the hymen may sometimes be seen covering all or part of the vaginal opening. Indeed, even upon entering the world, the hymen is only a partial barrier since menstrual liquid and different secretions have to have the option to leave the body regardless of whether or not there has been penile-vaginal intercourse. In this manner, a solid hymen cannot be regarded as proof of "virginity." Between the entrance of the urethra and the anus is where the vaginal aperture may be found. It is bordered on both sides by openings that lead to the Bartholin glands, also known as the larger vestibular glands.

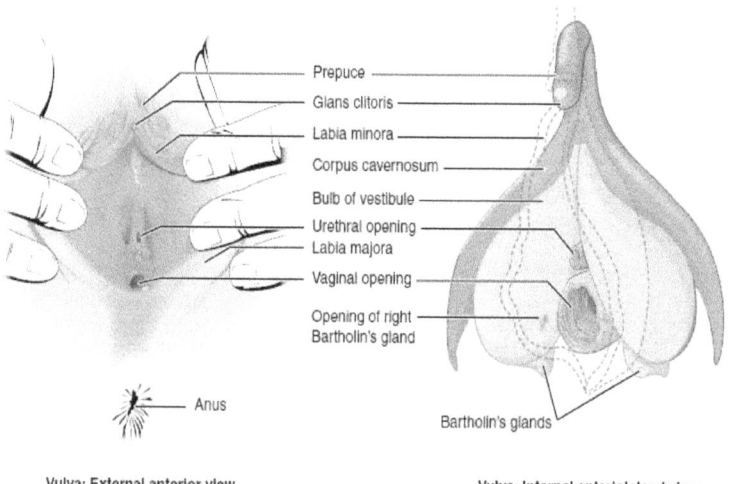

Figure 5.1: Vulva

5.1.2 Internal Female Genitalia

The vagina is a muscular tube that is roughly 10 centimeters in length and acts as the entrance to the reproductive system (see Figure 5.1). It is also the opening through which the contents of the uterus are expelled during menstruation and delivery of the baby. The vaginal orifice opening may be partly surrounded by the hymen, which is thin and perforated. A rupture of the hymen may occur as a result of vigorous physical activity, penile–vaginal intercourse, or the birthing process. Bodily fluid is delivered by the Bartholin's glands and the smaller vestibular glands, the two of which are situated near the clitoris. This bodily fluid assists with maintaining the dampness level in the vestibular locale.

A healthy population of microorganisms may be found in the vagina, and they play an important role in warding off infections caused by bacteria, yeast, and other organisms that have the potential to enter the vagina. Vaginal bacteria belonging to the genus Lactobacillus are the most common kind found in a woman who is in good health. This family of helpful bacteria flora produces lactic acid, which helps maintain an acidic pH, which in turn protects the vagina by keeping it healthy. In these acidic circumstances, the likelihood of potential pathogens surviving is decreased. The vagina is a self-cleansing organ because of the blend of lactic acid and other vaginal liquids. The practice of douching, which comprises of washing out the vagina with liquid, may upset the usual balance of good bacteria and actually increase a woman's gamble for infections and vaginal distress. In point of fact, the American School of Obstetricians and Gynecologists advises that ladies ought to refrain from doucheing in request to enable the vagina to have its usual healthy population of protecting microbial flora.

The ovaries are the female gonads (organ that produces female sex cells/eggs) and each one of them is about the size of an almond. It is the ovarian ligament, not the fallopian tubes, that associates the uterus to the ovaries. The ovaries are tracked down inside the pelvic cavity of the body.

The uterine cylinders, also known as fallopian cylinders or oviducts, are liable for providing a pathway for the ovum to go from the ovary to the uterus. Each of the two uterine cylinders is located in nearness to one of the ovaries, yet they don't link to it straightforwardly. In many cases, fertilization will take place in the part of the cylinder that is alluded to as the ampulla. Oocytes, in contrast to sperm, don't have flagella, and that means they are unable to independently move. The inquiry currently is the manner by which they make their way into the uterine cylinder and onward into the uterus. Contractions of the smooth muscle all the way down the length of the uterine cylinder are caused by high quantities of estrogen that happen around the hour of ovulation. A synchronized development that clears the surface of the ovary and the pelvic cavity is the outcome of these contractions, which take place each 4 to 8 seconds on average.

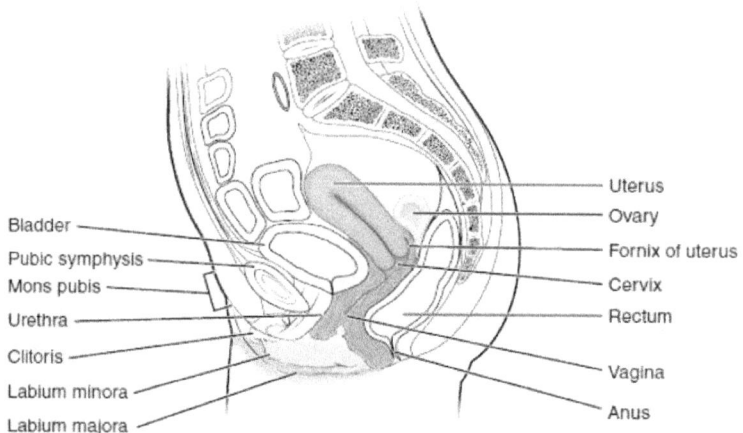

(a) Human female reproductive system: lateral view

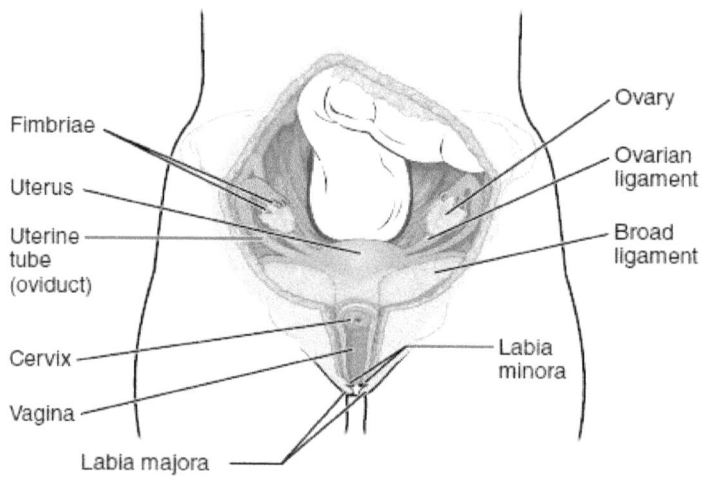

(b) Human female reproductive system: anterior view

Figure 5.2: Women's Reproductive System

On the off chance that the egg is treated, the ensuing zygote will start to part into two cells, then, at that point, four cells, and so on, as it travels down the uterine cylinder and into the uterus. This cycle will continue as lengthy as the pregnancy continues. There, it will start to grow again when it has implanted. On the off chance that the egg isn't treated, it will just deteriorate, either in the uterine cylinder or in the uterus, and then, at that point, it will be ousted with the following month of menstruation assuming it is in the uterus.

The uterus is a muscular organ that is liable for providing nourishment and backing for the developing fetus. At the point when a female isn't pregnant, its size is typically anywhere between 2 and 3 inches in length and width on average. It is separated into three parts. The point that is the most elevated overall is known as the fundus. The expression "assortment of uterus" alludes to the area of the uterus that is located in the middle. The cervix is the thin, protruding base part of the uterus that reaches out into the vagina. Affected by estrogen, the bodily fluid secretions delivered by the cervix transform into a thin and stringy consistency. This change in consistency may assist with expediting the transit of sperm through the reproductive framework.

There are three distinct layers that contain the uterine wall. The perimetrium, which is the external layer, the myometrium, which is the muscle layer, and the endometrium, of which a part is lost during menstruation. Myometrial tissue makes up the majority of the uterus, and its muscle filaments run in three unique bearings: horizontally, vertically, and diagonally. This arrangement makes it possible for the uterus to go through intense contractions during conveyance, as well as the less intense contractions (also known as cramps) that assist in the release of menstrual blood during a woman's period.

5.2 FEMALE REPRODUCTIVE PHYSIOLOGY

5.2.1 Menstruation

Each month, a woman's body goes through a process known as the menstrual cycle in which it prepares itself for the possibility of becoming pregnant. The length of time between the beginning of one period and the beginning of the following menstrual cycle is typically 28 days, however this number may vary anywhere from 21 days to 35 days. The duration of a period typically ranges from three to five days. In the United States, the average age at which a girl has her first period is 12, however the onset of menstruation may occur at any time between the ages of 8 and 16. Menarche is a word that refers to the first incidence of menstruation in adolescent females.

Menstruation is the process by which a woman's body rids itself of the uterine lining, which is a component of the endometrium. See the explanation of the menstrual cycle below for further information on how the blood from menstruation leaves the body via the vagina. Menstrual blood exits the body through the cervix through a tiny hole. The menstrual cycle refers to the pattern of regular occurrence of menstruation. A regular menstrual cycle is an indication that a person's reproductive systems are healthy and functioning normally. This cycle not only gets the body ready for pregnancy, but it also produces vital chemicals (hormones) that are used for a variety of physiological activities, some of which are connected to pregnancy and others of which are not.

In the main half of the cycle, there is a gradual increase in the amount of estrogen. Estrogen is essential to bone health and advances improvement and thickening in the lining of the uterus, which it does by acting as a development factor. In the event that a pregnancy creates, the embryo will get sustenance from this endometrial lining. A maturing ovum will take place in one of the ovaries at the same time as the lining of the belly is expanding. The egg is released from the ovary sometime around the fourteenth day of a typical 28-day cycle. Ovulation is the term for this interaction. After the egg has been released from the ovary, it continues its excursion to the uterus through the fallopian tube. The levels of certain chemicals increase, which assists in preparing the lining of the uterus for pregnancy. The three days leading up to a woman's ovulation, as well as the actual day, are the most ripe times for a woman to get pregnant. Remember that ladies whose menstrual cycles are more limited or longer than typical may encounter ovulation earlier or later than day 14 of their periods. At the point when an egg is prepared by a sperm cell from a man and then attaches itself to the uterine wall, the woman is said to be pregnant. At the point when an egg isn't prepared, chemical levels fall, and the uterine lining that was thickened because of pregnancy is shed during the month to month menstrual cycle.

The process of vascularization takes place in the endometrial lining of the uterus during a regular menstrual cycle. This is one of the steps in the menstrual cycle. In preparation for the possibility that the egg will be discharged and fertilized during this cycle, the lining of the uterus will thicken and become more blood-rich during this phase. Tiny blood vessels will multiply. In the event that this does not occur, the lining of the uterus is lost, which results in a monthly period.

- **Implantation**

If pregnancy is achieved, the fertilized egg, now known as the embryo, makes its way into the endometrium, the tissue from which the pregnant person's piece of the placenta, known as the decidua basalis, will eventually form.

Implantation, often alluded to as nidation, is the stage in the improvement of mammalian embryos wherein the blastocyst hatches, attaches, adheres, and invades into the wall of the female's uterus. This stage is also known as the implantation stage. The implantation of the treated egg into the uterine wall is the most vital phase during the time spent becoming pregnant. Assuming this step is effective, the woman is said to be pregnant. The presence of elevated degrees of human chorionic gonadotropin (hCG) in a woman's body during a pregnancy test enables the embryo to be distinguished as having been implanted. In request for the embryo to foster appropriately after implantation, it will be furnished with oxygen and sustenance. There is a large amount of diversity among the various species of mammals with regard to the kinds of trophoblast cells that are present and the structures that make up the placenta. The first four phases of implantation, out of a total of five recognized stages of implantation, including two pre-implantation stages that come before placentation, are comparable across all species. Migration and hatching are the first two steps, followed by pre-contact, attachment, adhesion, and finally invasion. The pre-implantation embryo is connected to the first and second phases of the pre-implantation process.

In humans, the process of implantation starts around four to five days after fertilization, after the stage of hatching that occurs approximately four to five days after fertilization. The blastocyst will have just a superficial attachment to the lining of the uterus by the time the first week is through. The process of implantation is finished by the time the second week is through.

- **Gestation**

The uterus expands during a woman's pregnancy, and as it does so, the muscle walls around it get thinner. This process is analogous to that of a balloon being inflated. This makes space for both the growing baby and the amniotic fluid, which helps protect it. First, the pregnant woman produces amniotic fluid, and then, later, the baby contributes urine and lung secretions to the production of amniotic fluid.

- **Labor**

In order to get ready for labor and delivery, the muscular layer of the uterus starts to contract intermittently while the woman is pregnant. These "practice" contractions, also known as Braxton-Hick's contractions, are quite similar to the cramping that occurs during menstruation; nonetheless, some people are completely unaware that they are occurring. Labor contractions, in contrast to Braxton-Hick's contractions, get dynamically more intense and are sufficiently strong to compel the baby out of the uterus and into the vagina. Following the conveyance of a baby, the uterus will continue to contract in request to facilitate the conveyance of the placenta. In the following weeks, it will continue to contract in request to lessen the size of the uterus to its generally expected level and stopped the bleeding that happens in the uterus because of conveyance.

Signs that you're about to receive period

Menstruation symptoms might be experienced or not experienced by different individuals. The severity of these symptoms might also differ from person to person. Cramps are the most typical manifestation of this condition. Your uterus is contracting in order to expel its lining, which is causing the cramping you experience in your pelvic region.

Additional indications that your menstruation is coming include the following:

- Mood swings are common.
- Trouble sleeping.
- Headache.
- Urge or desire for food.
- Bloating.
- Breast tenderness.
- Acne.

5.2.2 The Menstruation cycle

After reaching pubescence, all females generate mature egg cells once a month during an interaction known as the menstrual cycle. This interaction is also known as the reproductive cycle. During this time, an ovary will release a completely evolved egg, which will then, at that point, make its way to the uterus. In the event that the egg doesn't get prepared in the uterus, the lining of the uterine sheds away, and the reproductive cycle starts over again. Although the average length of a menstrual cycle is 28 days, it is possible for certain ladies' periods to be under 21 days or longer than 35 days. The endocrine framework is liable for regulating the entire menstrual cycle, and the chemicals that play a job in this interaction include follicle-stimulating chemical (FSH), luteinizing chemical (LH), estrogen, and progesterone. The pituitary gland is liable for the creation of both the FSH and LH chemicals, while the ovaries are answerable for the development of estrogen and progesterone chemicals.

In addition to hormonal imbalances, the disruption in the menstrual cycle may also be caused by a large number of other reasons. These can all play a role in the condition. Diet, physical activity, mental stress, and overall body weight, as well as growth or decrease, may all have an impact on a woman's menstrual cycle. There is a possibility that the cycle may become erratic at times, particularly throughout adolescence. If a woman is not pregnant, her menstrual cycle will repeat every month from the time she reaches adolescence until she is between the ages of 45 and 55. Once a woman reaches the age of 55, her ovaries begin to slow down the rate at which they produce hormone and release mature eggs. As time goes on, the woman will no longer have menstrual cycles; as a result, she will lose the ability to have children.

- The principal day of a menstruation is always viewed as Day 1. This happens when chemical levels decline at the finish of the past cycle, which conveys a message to blood and tissues lining the uterus to break down and be ousted from the body. During this time, a woman may or may not have menstruation. The bleeding often lasts for around five days.
- In most cases, the bleeding will cease by the seventh day. In the weeks leading up to this point, hormones stimulate fluid-filled sacs on the surface of the ovaries to form in the form of follicles. Every follicle has one egg inside of it.

- From day 7 to day 14, a single follicle will continue to mature into an adult stage of development. In preparation for the implantation of an egg that has been fertilized, the lining of the uterus begins to thicken. The lining contains a lot of blood as well as other nutrients.
- Ovulation is the interaction by which an egg is released from the ovary after a mature follicle has been stimulated by chemicals to break. This happens around Day 14 of a 28-day cycle.
- The egg will continue its excursion toward the uterus throughout the following not many days as it travels through the fallopian tube. In the event that the egg is treated by a sperm, it will travel via the fallopian tube and attach itself to the lining of the uterus. This happens provided that fertilization happens.
- Around day 25, chemical levels will begin to diminish in the event that the egg doesn't get prepared. This indicates that the following menstrual cycle will start without further ado. The egg will be lost related to the resulting menstruation.

The activity of the hormones produced by the ovaries and the anterior pituitary gland, as well as the changes that occur as a direct consequence of those hormones in the uterus and ovaries, are all components of the menstrual cycle. All of them are combined into, which may seem confusing at first, but you should refer to it as you read the following.

To begin with, it is important to take note of the four chemicals that are involved. Follicle stimulating chemical (FSH) and luteinizing chemical (LH) come from the anterior pituitary gland, estrogen comes from the ovarian follicle, and progesterone comes from the corpus luteum. The changes in levels of these chemicals are displayed here as they would take place throughout a typical 28-day cycle. A cycle may be separated into three distinct parts, which are the menstrual phase, the follicular phase, and the luteal phase.

The maturation of the gathering of tertiary follicles in the ovary, the development and resulting shedding of the endometrial lining in the uterus, and the capability of the uterine cylinders and vagina all add to the three phases of the menstrual cycle, the succession of changes where the uterine lining sheds, revamps, and prepares for implantation.

The menstrual cycle begins with the principal day of menstruation, also known as day one of a woman's period. Counting the quantity of days between the onsets of hemorrhage in two sequential cycles yields the cycle length. Considering that the average duration of a woman's menstrual cycle is 28 days, this period is utilized to determine the scheduling of occasions within the cycle. Notwithstanding, the duration of a woman's menstrual cycle can vary from 21 to 32 days, depending on the woman and her cycle.

5.2.2.1 Phases of Menstruation Cycle

The same chemicals that "drive" the follicular and luteal phases of the ovarian cycle are also answerable for the three distinct phases of the menstrual cycle. There are three phases: menstruation, proliferation, and secretion.

1. Menses Phase

The shedding of the lining happens during the time of the menstrual cycle known as the menses phase. This phase relates to the days when a woman will have menstruation. Although it typically lasts for around five days, the menstruation time frame may last anywhere from two to seven days or much longer. Because the degrees of progesterone, follicle stimulating chemical (FSH), and luteinizing chemical (LH) are low all through this phase of the ovarian cycle, menstruation takes place at this time. It is important to remember that the degeneration of the corpus luteum, which signals the finish of the luteal phase, causes concentrations of progesterone to fall. This decrease in progesterone causes the stratum functionalis of the endometrium to shed because of the cycle.

2. Proliferative Phase

After the progression of menstruation has halted, the endometrium will start to develop a new, signaling the beginning of the time of the menstrual cycle known as the proliferative phase. It manifests itself when the granulosa and theca cells of the tertiary follicles start producing elevated degrees of estrogen. The endometrial lining is stimulated to regenerate because of this increase in estrogen levels.

Recall that high estrogen concentrations will ultimately lead to a drop in FSH as an outcome of negative feedback, which will bring about atresia of all of the growing tertiary follicles with the exception of one of them. The transition from negative feedback to positive feedback, which takes place when the dominant follicle delivers a higher amount of estrogen, then encourages the LH flood that will cause ovulation to take place. Ovulation takes place on day

14 of a menstrual cycle that lasts for a usual 28 days. The finish of the proliferative phase and the follicular phase is signaled by ovulation in the female reproductive cycle.

3. Secretory Phase

In addition to causing a rise in LH levels, elevated estrogen levels cause an increase in the contractions of the uterine tube, which makes it easier to collect and move the egg that has been ovulated. High estrogen levels also have the impact of somewhat lowering the vaginal acidity, which creates a climate that is more welcoming to sperm. The luteal phase of the ovarian cycle begins when the granulosa cells of the collapsed follicle in the ovary go through the course of luteinization. This marks the beginning of the corpus luteum, which is answerable for releasing progesterone. Progesterone got from the corpus luteum starts off the secretory phase of the menstrual cycle in the uterus. This is the time of the cycle wherein the endometrial lining becomes ready for implantation. The endometrial glands will continue to produce a liquid that is high in glycogen for the following ten to twelve days. Assuming fertilization has taken place, the circle of cells that is currently forming from the zygote will be fed by this liquid. At the same time, the spiral arteries develop so they may give blood to the stratum functionalis that has become thicker.

Assuming there is no pregnancy within ten to twelve days, the corpus luteum will transform into the corpus albicans. This interaction takes place naturally. Both estrogen and progesterone levels will decrease, and the endometrium will turn out to be less thick subsequently. There will be a secretion of prostaglandins, which will create a narrowing of the spiral arteries and a decrease in the conveyance of oxygen. Endometrial tissue will eventually die, which will bring about menstruation or the beginning of the resulting cycle.

5.2.2.2 Phases of a normal menstrual cycle.

1. Menstrual phase

Menstruation, often known as menses, is the process of the functional layer of the endometrium being shed throughout a woman's reproductive years. In spite of the fact that this marks the conclusion of a woman's menstrual cycle, it is still a good place to begin since the beginning of menstruation can be identified with relative ease. The duration of menstruation may range from two days to eight days, with three to six days being the norm. During this time period, there is an increase in the amount of FSH that is secreted, and various ovarian follicles begin to form.

2. Follicular phase

The improvement of ovarian follicles and the release of estrogen by follicle cells are both encouraged by the chemical FSH. The amount of LH that is secreted is similarly growing, however at a more slow rate. FSH and estrogen are both answerable for fostering the turn of events and maturity of the ovum. Estrogen also encourages the creation of veins in the endometrium, which assists with repairing the functional layer. This phase reaches a resolution with ovulation, which happens when an unexpected ascent in LH sets off the crack of a mature ovarian follicle.

On the main day of your menstruation, this phase begins. The following things take place during the follicular phase of the menstrual cycle:

Your brain releases two chemicals, follicle stimulating chemical (FSH) and luteinizing chemical (LH), which go via your blood to your ovaries.

Each egg in your ovaries fills in its own "shell," or follicle, because of the chemicals. This number ranges from 15 to 20 eggs.

The union of the chemical estrogen is similarly increased by these chemicals (FSH and LH).

Follicle-stimulating chemical union is turned off when estrogen levels increase. The body may control the quantity of follicles that will mature eggs for release via carefully balancing its chemical levels.

One follicle in one ovary becomes dominant as the follicular phase creates and continues to mature. All of different follicles in the gathering are smothered by one dominating follicle. They along these lines cease developing and pass away. Estrogen continues to be delivered by the dominant follicle.

3. Ovulatory phase

It takes around 14 days for the ovulatory phase, also known as ovulation, to begin after the follicular phase has begun, however the precise date might vary. The ovulatory phase is the second phase of your menstrual cycle. This period lasts for around 24 hours. The majority of women will get their first period anywhere from 10 to 16 days following ovulation. The following occurrences will take place at this stage:

- The increase in estrogen that results from the dominant follicle causes your brain to create a greater quantity of luteinizing hormone (LH), which leads to increased fertility.
- Because of this, the egg that was contained inside the dominant follicle is released from the ovary.
- During the process known as ovulation, the egg is retrieved by projections that look like fingers and are located at the end of the fallopian tubes. These are termed fimbriae. Eggs are transported into the fallopian tube by means of the fimbriae.
- Many ladies and people AFAB may see an increase in egg white cervical bodily fluid beginning one day and lasting anywhere from one to five days before to ovulation. This bodily fluid is the vaginal discharge that serves to trap and sustain a sperm on its path to meet the egg in request to treat it. It does this by acting as a barrier between the sperm and the egg.

4. Luteal phase

The ruptured follicle, when stimulated by the hormone LH, transforms into the corpus luteum and starts to produce progesterone in addition to the hormone estrogen. Progesterone encourages the storage of nutrients like glycogen and promotes further expansion of blood vessels in the functional layer of the endometrium. This proliferation of blood vessels is stimulated by progesterone. As the level of progesterone production rises, the level of LH secretion falls. However, if the ovum does not get fertilized, the level of progesterone secretion will also begin to fall. It is impossible to sustain the endometrium in the absence of progesterone, which causes it to begin shedding during menstruation. The release of FSH starts to go up (while the levels of estrogen and progesterone go down), and the cycle starts all over again. In addition, the hormones inhibin and relaxin are released by the corpus luteum throughout the course of a cycle. The anterior pituitary gland, which produces FSH and maybe LH as well, is inhibited in its release of these hormones by inhibitn. It is expected that relaxin, in the same way as progesterone does, would slow the contractions of the myometrium, which will assist in the successful implantation of the early embryo. The cycle lasts for an average of 28 days. The standard range for the length of a woman's menstrual cycle is between 23 and 35 days. Ladies who participate in lively activity for expanded timeframes have an increased gamble of developing amenorrhea, sometimes known as the cessation of menstruation. Apparently this is associated with a decrease in overall muscle to fat ratio. Apparently the reproductive cycle reaches a conclusion on the off chance that a woman needs more energy saves for both herself and a fetus that is forming inside of her. Right now, the exact cycle by which anything like this takes place isn't totally known. Amenorrhea is a condition that may happen related to times of physical or mental pressure, anorexia nervosa, or a variety of endocrine diseases.

Following ovulation, the luteal phase starts and includes the following activities:

- The void ovarian follicle transforms into a brand-new construction known as the corpus luteum after it discharges its egg.
- The chemicals progesterone and estrogen are secreted by the corpus luteum. Your uterus becomes ready for a prepared egg to implant thanks to progesterone.
- On the off chance that there has been sexual activity and the egg has been treated (origination), the embryo will pass through your fallopian cylinder and implant in your uterus. Pregnancy starts very much like this.
- The egg disintegrates in your uterus on the off chance that it isn't treated. The lining of your uterus sheds and disintegrates when keeping a pregnancy is not generally needed. This is the start of your menstruation.

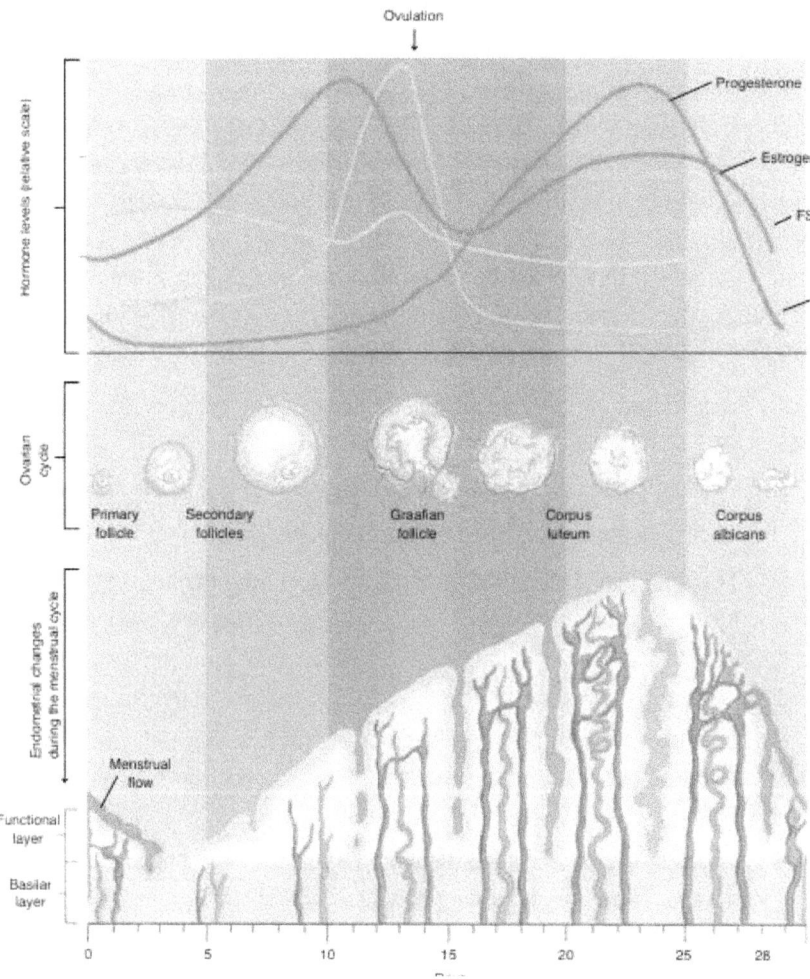

Figure 5.3: The menstrual cycle. The levels of the important hormones are shown relative to one another throughout the cycle

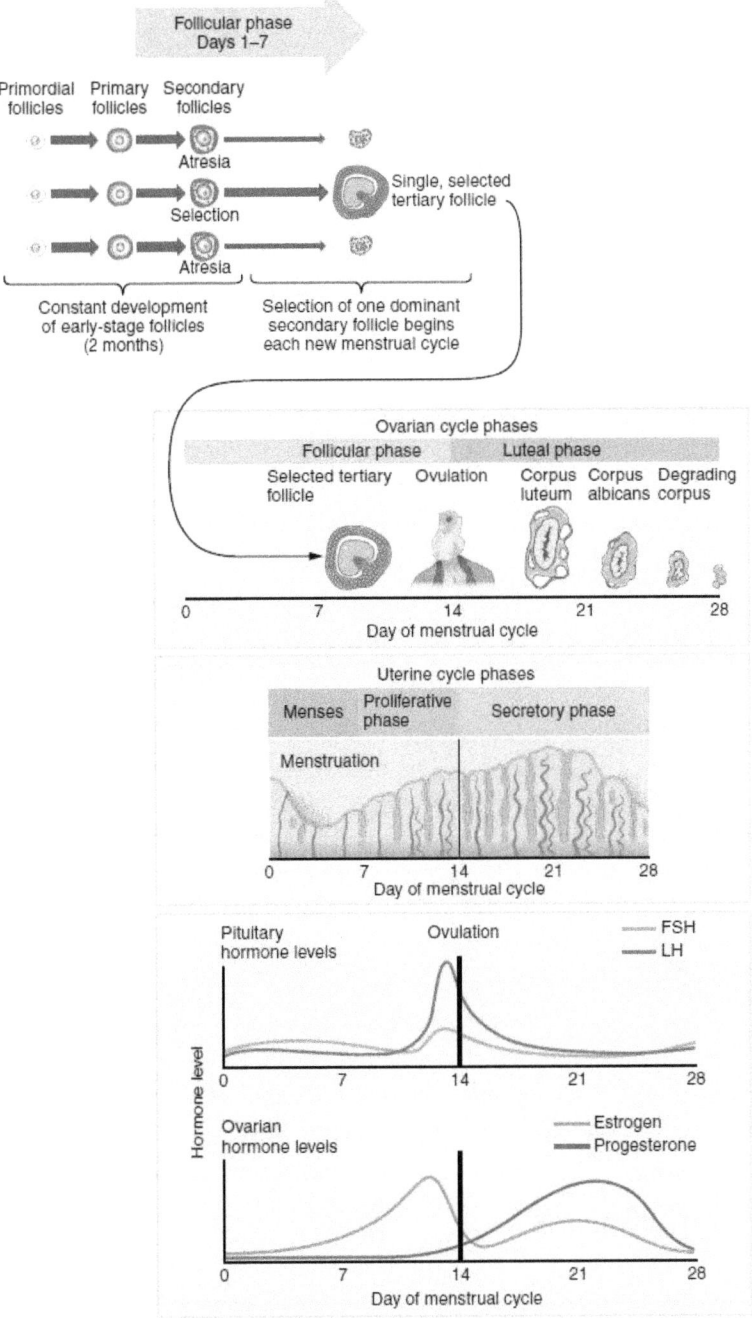

Figure 5.4: Ovarian and Menstrual Hormones

5.2.3 Four major hormones in the menstrual cycle

The menstrual cycle is constrained by a combination of the actions of four primary chemicals, which are defined as "chemicals that stimulate or regulate the activity of cells or organs." The following chemicals are included:

1. Estrogen

An essential sex chemical for sustaining sexual and reproductive health is estrogen. Your normal pattern of menstruation and menopause cause changes in your estrogen levels. Estrogen levels that are reliably high or low could indicate an issue that has to be addressed by your PCP.

There is a gathering of sex chemicals known as estrogens or oestrogens (see the changes in spelling), and these chemicals are important for the turn of events and control of the female reproductive framework as well as secondary sex characteristics. There are three primary endogenous estrogens that are liable for the creation of estrogenic chemicals. These are estrone (E1), estradiol (E2), and estriol (E3). The most remarkable and broadly disseminated estrane is known as estradiol. Estestrol, also known as E4, is an additional kind of estrogen that is only created during pregnancy.

Estrogens are delivered endogenously in all vertebrates and in many insect species. The fact that estrogenic sex chemicals are found in the two vertebrates and insects hints to a very lengthy evolutionary history for these chemicals. All kinds of people have quantitatively lower quantities of estrogens circulating in their bodies compared to androgens. Although the quantities of estrogen found in folks are far lower than those found in females, the chemical nonetheless plays a crucial capability in the male body's physiological cycles. Estrogens are able to pass through the cell membrane, very much like the other steroid chemicals easily. Whenever they have entered the phone, they attach to estrogen receptors (emergency rooms) and activate them, which in turn changes the outflow of countless genes.In addition, estrogens bind to rapid-signaling membrane estrogen receptors (mERs), like GPER (GPR30), and activate these receptors.

In addition to their function as naturally occurring hormones, estrogens also have a place in the medical field, where they are used in the treatment of menopausal symptoms, the administration of hormonal contraceptives, and the administration of feminizing hormone therapy to transgender women and nonbinary persons. Xenoestrogens are the collective name given to both naturally occurring and synthetic estrogens that have been discovered in the environment. Estrogens are one example of the diverse class of chemicals known as endocrine-disrupting compounds (EDCs), which are known to be harmful to human and animal health and to disrupt normal reproductive function.

Types of estrogen

There are primarily three different kinds of estrogen:

a. **Estrone (E1)** is the predominant kind of estrogen that continues to be produced by your body after the menopause.
b. **Estradiol (E2)** is the predominant type of estrogen that will be found in your body while you are sexually active. It is the most powerful version of the female hormone estrogen..
c. **Estriol (E3)** is the predominant kind of estrogen seen in a pregnant woman.

2. Follicle-stimulating hormone

Follicle-stimulating hormone, sometimes known as FSH, is a gonadotropin. This kind of hormone is a glycoprotein polypeptide. The gonadotropic cells of the anterior pituitary gland are answerable for the union and secretion of FSH, which is then liable for regulating the cycles of improvement, development, pubertal maturation, and propagation in the body. In the reproductive framework, the luteinizing hormone (LH) and follicle stimulating hormone (FSH) act together.

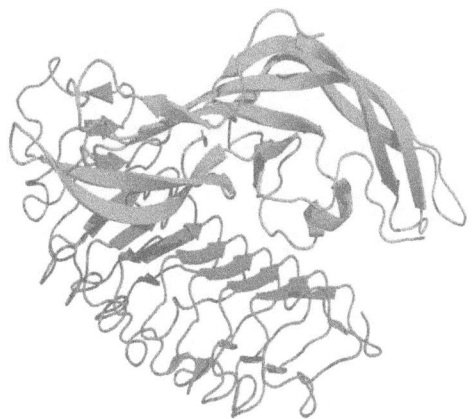

Figure 5.5: Follicle-stimulating hormone (FSH)

Function of follicle-stimulating hormone (FSH)?

Follicle-stimulating hormone is an essential hormone that serves a variety of purposes, all of which are determined by the sort of sexual organs (gonads) a person has in addition to their age.

a. The role of FSH in fetal development

The pituitary gland of the fetus produces luteinizing hormone (LH) and free somatotropin (FSH) consistently and third trimesters of pregnancy (week 13 to the furthest limit of week 26 and week 27 to the furthest limit of the pregnancy, individually). As the fetus' most memorable ovarian follicle or seminiferous tubule (curled tubules inside the testicles) matures, these hormone levels reach their peak in the center of pregnancy.

b. FSH activity throughout puberty

Kids often have low FSH levels. Gonadotropin-releasing hormone (GnRH), which causes FSH and LH to be released, is created by the hypothalamus as adolescence approaches (often between the ages of 10 and 14). The transition to sexual maturity and advancement starts at this point.

Together, FSH and LH cause the testicles of males or kids who were assigned male upon entering the world (AMAB) to start releasing testosterone. This hormone is in charge of both sperm creation and the outward manifestations of pubescence, like the improvement of body hair and a more profound voice.

FSH and LH cause the ovaries of females or youngsters who were designated female upon entering the world (AFAB) to start generating estrogen. Pubescence related materially changes including breast development and menstruation are welcomed on by this hormone.

c. FSH activity in menstruation individuals who were born as females (AFAB)

The primary job of FSH in ladies or AFAB who are menstruation is to assist in controlling the menstrual cycle. FSH specifically encourages the development of follicles on the ovary to prepare the eggs for ovulation. The follicles start to deliver estrogen and a little amount of progesterone into your blood as they become greater.

A stage of the menstrual cycle is ovulation. About day 14 of a 28-day menstrual cycle is the point at which it happens. Ovulation is specifically the release of an egg (ovum) from an ovary.

Consistently, between days six and fourteen of the menstrual cycle, the hormone FSH sets off the maturation of follicles in one of the ovaries. In any case, from days 10 to 14, only one of the growing follicles delivers an egg that is completely evolved. The mature follicle explodes and releases its egg at about day 14 of the menstrual cycle because of an abrupt ascent in LH (ovulation).

Following ovulation, the burst follicle forms into the corpus luteum, a transient endocrine gland that secretes a ton of progesterone. The uterine lining is assisted with becoming ready for pregnancy by progesterone, which inhibits the development of FSH.

The five-day excursion of the egg via the fallopian cylinder to the uterus starts. On the off chance that a sperm prepares an egg effectively at this time, pregnancy will follow. The corpus luteum degrades at the finish of the cycle in the event that there is no fertilization. At the point when FSH levels start to rise again, progesterone creation starts to decline and the ensuing menstrual cycle — your period — starts.

d. FSH function in those who were born as males (AMAB)

FSH advances sperm creation in males or those with AMAB. FSH upholds sperm creation related to testosterone, which is stimulated by LH within the testicles.

1. Luteinizing hormone

Your body produces luteinizing hormone (LH), a substance that regulates key reproductive framework capabilities. LH advances ovulation and aids in the creation of the hormones expected to sustain pregnancy. On the off chance that you are experiencing irregular menstruation or reproductive issues, your PCP may ask for a test to measure your LH levels.

Luteinizing hormone (also known as luteinising hormone, lutropin, and occasionally lutrophin) is a hormone that is generated by gonadotropic cells in the anterior pituitary gland. Different names for this hormone are luteinizing hormone (LH), luteinizing hormone, and lutropin. The gonadotropin-releasing hormone (GnRH) that is released from the hypothalamus controls the amount of LH that is created. Ovulation and the development of the corpus luteum are both initiated in females when there is an abrupt increase in LH levels, often known as a LH flood. In men, where LH was previously known as interstitial cell-stimulating hormone (ICSH), it is answerable for boosting the creation of testosterone by the Leydig cells. Together with follicle-stimulating hormone (also known as FSH), it has a synergistic impact.

Luteinizing hormone in women or DFAB

Your ovaries are stimulated by LH to go through alterations that advance pregnancy and sustain your month to month cycle. Individuals who were brought into the world with the designation "female" (DFAB) experience these alterations because of LH, including cisgender ladies, certain transgender males, and nonbinary individuals with vagina.

a. **Ovulation:** Around the second seven day stretch of each menstrual cycle, a spike in LH sets off the release of a mature egg from your ovary. You're at the point in your cycle when you're probably going to get pregnant assuming your LH level is high at this time.

b. **Progesterone production:** During the third and fourth significant length of your menstrual cycle, LH stimulates the corpus luteum, a part of your ovary, to create more progesterone. A hormone called progesterone is supposed to maintain a pregnancy in its early stages.

LH levels rise when estrogen and progesterone levels fall as you become more seasoned and go through menopause.

2. Progesterone

The main capability of progesterone is to prepare the endometrium, or uterine lining, for the development and implantation of a treated egg. Assuming there is no pregnancy during your menstrual cycle, the endometrium sheds. Assuming that fertilization happens, progesterone increases to maintain the pregnancy.

Progesterone and menstruation

Ovulation, the cycle in which an egg is released from the ovary, often takes place sometime in the center of a woman's menstrual cycle. The vacant egg follicle brings about the formation of the corpus luteum, which thereafter starts the creation of progesterone. Your corpus luteum is a transitory gland that advances the beginning of a pregnancy in the event that origination happens during that cycle. On the off chance that you get pregnant, your cycle will begin with your corpus luteum already present. Your uterine lining will get thicker because of taking progesterone, which will make it easier for a treated egg to implant in your uterus.

If during that cycle an egg is not fertilized, which means that you do not get pregnant, the corpus luteum will break down, which will result in a fall in the levels of progesterone. Your uterine lining will begin to weaken and break down as your progesterone levels drop, which will result in the start of your period.

Progesterone during pregnancy

If an egg is prepared by sperm and pregnancy takes place, the corpus luteum doesn't degrade and instead continues to create additional progesterone. Your uterine lining is thick and loaded with veins, which supplies the prepared egg (which is currently an embryo) with the supplements it necessities to develop. The manufacturing of progesterone will be taken up by the placenta after it has shaped.

Progesterone levels rise gradually during pregnancy, climbing to their maximum point in the third trimester (weeks 28–40 of the pregnancy). Progesterone levels remain elevated after delivery. The years leading up to menopause, when ovulation finally ends, are associated with a fall in progesterone levels.

Estrogen and Progesterone

The ovaries are answerable for the creation of the hormone's estrogen and progesterone, which advance the improvement of reproductive organs by ensuring that the uterine cycle is functioning appropriately and by fostering the advancement of female secondary sex characteristics. The uterine cycle is terminated and the ovaries cease creation of estrogen and progesterone hormones when a woman reaches menopause, which typically happens between the ages of 45 and 55.

Hormones are the chemical messengers of the body, and they function by flowing through the circulation to convey instructions to cells that are adapted to accept their signals. Hormones are responsible for a variety of physiological processes. Even though each hormone has a unique role, estrogen and progesterone are both considered to be members of the same category of hormones that are referred to as sex hormones.

These hormones have a role in reproduction and have an effect on the development of sexuality throughout adolescence. They undergo continuous change over the course of your cycle (unless you use a certain form of hormonal birth control), and a person's levels continue to alter even after they reach adulthood.

In women, the ovaries are primarily responsible for the production of estrogen and progesterone. These hormones have a variety of effects, including the regulation of puberty and the growth of breasts, as well as the capacity to conceive children and the growth of body hair.

Estrogen affects not just bone health and cardiovascular function but also brain function, skin tissue health, and cardiovascular function in addition to its more common association with menstruation. It is predominantly the hormone progesterone that is responsible for preparing your body for pregnancy and then for sustaining that pregnancy once it has begun. It is essential to keep in mind that estrogen and progesterone are not characteristics that are exclusive to women or to those who experience menstruation. Other individuals, however, maybe do not have ovaries or do not have an egg that is actively produced every month. As a result, their hormone supply is created in other places of the body such as the adrenal glands or adipose tissues.

5.3 SEXUAL RESPONSE CYCLE AND FERTILITY

Let us take into consideration the sexual reaction cycle, which is a research-based paradigm formulated by Masters and Johnson (1966). They named it after themselves. The sexual reaction cycle is an idea that defines the three stages that the majority of individuals go through when they participate in sexual intercourse. These three phases include excitation, plateau, and climax. Both Masters and Johnson were eager to stress out that every person had a one-of-a-kind and distinct sexual reaction, going so far as to say that no two sexual experiences between the same individuals could be anticipated to be completely similar to one another. In spite of this, these three stages are quite typical for the majority of individuals.

When sexual interaction starts, both males and females go through the same three stages of sexual development. During the excitement phase, blood travels to the pelvis, bringing with it an increase in the amount of lymphatic fluid and plasma present in the area. The penis, vaginal walls, and clitoris are some of the areas of the sexual anatomy that are most likely to swell up as a result of hormonal and psychological stressors. While this is taking place, the plateau phase starts. This is when more hormones are delivered, the body creates more dampness, the heart rate increases, and the intensity of tangible experience (including contact, smell, sight, and hearing) increases. During the orgasm phase, an electrical development of energy is released, which is related with a musical contraction of the pelvic floor muscles, the urine and anal sphincters, and various glands for men. This contraction also causes a release of endorphins, which are neurotransmitters that make you feel far better. This experience is known as an orgasm. Goal is the cycle that allows the sexual apparatus to return to its state before stimulation after an orgasmic experience has finished.

Fertilization and Pregnancy

After implantation takes place, maternal and fetal tissues come together to form the placenta, which is responsible for the production of human chorionic gonadotropin (HCG). HCG is a hormone that keeps the level of corpus luteum in the ovary stable until the placenta starts releasing its own progesterone and estrogen hormones.

The process of fertilization begins with the attachment of the sperm head to the zona pellucida of the egg, which is the first step of the process. A successful fertilization will result in the restoration of the complete set of 46 chromosomes, which will then lead to the beginning of the development of an embryo. The process of fertilization consists of a few different phases. The initial step in the process is for the sperm to recognize the egg. The subsequent process is the control of how many sperm are allowed to enter the egg. It is impossible for numerous sperm to penetrate an egg because of a chain of critical molecular processes that are collectively referred to as the polyspermy block. In tandem with the process of fertilization, the egg undergoes the completion of the second meiotic division, which results in the expulsion of the second polar body. At this stage, the male and female pronuclei come together to form a single nucleus, which is then followed by the beginning of the first round of mitotic cell division.

Certain glycoproteins that perform the function of sperm receptors may be found in the zona pellucida. They do this by preventing the fusion of incompatible sperm cells (such as those from a different species) with the egg in a selective manner. The acrosome response, which is necessary for sperm penetration, is triggered when the sperm and egg come into contact with one another. It is possible for the sperm to navigate their way through the cumulus (granulosa) cells that surround the egg as a result of the release of proteolytic enzymes by the sperm. These enzymes disintegrate the matrix of the cumulus cells. This procedure, which may take up to half an hour, involves the sperm penetrating the zona pellucida with the assistance of proteolytic enzymes and the propelling power provided by the tail. After passing through the perivitelline gap, the head of the sperm attaches itself to the plasma membrane of the egg, and the microvilli that extend from the oolemma, which is the plasma membrane of the egg, reach out and encircle the sperm. This is the process that results in fertilization. After being swallowed up by the oolemma, the sperm finally have their whole heads and subsequently their tails absorbed into the ooplasm.

Cortical granules, which are organelles that are similar to lysosomes and are positioned below the oolemma, are released not long after the sperm has entered the egg. The cortical granules combine with the oolemma during this process. The process of fusion starts at the place where the sperm is attached to the egg and then spreads across the whole egg surface. The contents of the granules leak out into the perivitelline space and diffuse into the zona pellucida, which causes the zona response. This reaction is characterized by an inactivation of the sperm receptor and a thickening of the zona. As a consequence of this, polyspermia is avoided after the initial spermatozoon has set off the zona response since subsequent sperm are unable to pass through the zona after it has been activated.

A female's sexual reaction would normally follow a pattern that is similar to the one that follows:

- **Excitement phase:** The vaginal cavity becomes more swollen as a result of the presence of blood and lymphatic fluid. The uterus is lifted away from the pubic bone as a result of the secretion of hormones, which cause the uterus to go through moderate contractions. The labia get larger, and the clitoris thickens and contracts. Dampness is secreted by the vaginal tissues, and the actual vagina protracts and broadens somewhat inward during this phase. The energy phase, also known as the arousal phase or the main fervor phase, is the primary stage of the human sexual reaction cycle. This stage happens as an immediate result of a physical or mental suggestive improvement that leads to sexual arousal, for example, kissing, making out, daydreaming, or watching hot pictures. The body gets ready for sexual activity during this period, which ultimately leads to the plateau phase. With regards to inclinations for the duration of foreplay and the stimulation strategies that are used, there is a significant amount of socio-cultural variety. During foreplay, establishing at least some early arousal often involves a combination of physical and emotional association as well as stimulation of the erogenous zones.

- ***Excitement in both sexes:*** - In people of both sexes, the excitement phase is accompanied by a quickening of the pulse rate and the breathing rate, in addition to an increase in blood pressure. These changes occur simultaneously. The results of a survey that was carried out in 2006 indicate that direct stimulation of the nipples either initiates sexual arousal in roughly 82% of young females or amplifies it in approximately 52% of young men. Only 7–8% of those who responded said that it caused their sexual drive to decrease. Vasoconstriction of the skin, more often known as the sex flush, will occur in around fifty percent to seventy five percent of females and twenty five percent of men. Women are more likely to experience this phenomenon than males. Under warmer conditions, the sex flush has a larger likelihood of occurring; yet, it is conceivable that it will not emerge at all under colder conditions. Warmer conditions have a greater possibility of causing the sex flush to occur. The formation of pinkish patches under the breasts is the main indication of the female sex flush, which then, at that point, dynamically spreads to the breasts, chest, cheeks, hands, bottoms of the feet, and occasionally the entire body. This condition is sometimes alluded to as the "female sex flush." During sexual stimulation, vasocongestion, which is created by increased blood stream, adds to the darkening of the clitoris and the walls of the vagina. This happens because of increased blood stream. Although the shade of the skin during the male sex flush grows less reliably than it does in the female, it often starts in the epigastrium (upper gut), gets across the chest, and then continues to the neck, face, forehead, back, and sometimes the shoulders and forearms. In females, the shade of the skin during the sex flush grows more reliably than it does in males. It doesn't take long for the sex flush to disappear after an orgasmic experience, however it could last for as long as two hours, and in certain instances, you could also feel intense sweating at the same time. Generally speaking, the sex flush doesn't last extremely lengthy. The majority of the time, the request where the cards are taken out from the flush is the exact inverse of the request where they were dealt into the flush.[2] During this time span, individuals of the two genders go through an increase in the muscular tone (myotonia) of certain muscle gatherings. It is possible for an individual to deliberately or involuntarily experience this ascent in muscular tone. this has to be explained in more detail] In addition, the external anal sphincter may randomly contract in light of touch, or it may do so later on during orgasm in any event, when there is no contact between the partners.

- ***Excitement in females:*** - The excitation phase may persist for few minutes in females all the way up to several hours in males. The clitoris, the labia minora, and the vagina all swell up when vasoconstriction first begins to manifest in a woman. As the uterus rises and expands in size, the muscle that covers the vaginal entrance begins to contract, making the aperture smaller. A lubricating organic liquid is produced by the vaginal walls when the vaginal canal opens. While this is going on, the breasts become a little bit bigger, and the nipples get more defined and stand up straight.

- **Plateau phase:** The labia and clitoris get completely enlarged as the excitement continues, and the uterus becomes raised as a result of this. After the vagina has been stretched farther into the body, the lubrication is cut off shortly before the orgasm. The excitation phase may persist for few minutes in females all the way up to several hours in males. The clitoris, the labia minora, and the vagina all swell up when vasoconstriction first begins to manifest in a woman. As the uterus rises and expands in size, the muscle that covers the vaginal entrance begins to contract, making the aperture smaller. A lubricating organic liquid is produced by the vaginal walls when the vaginal canal opens. While this is going on, the breasts become a little bit bigger, and the nipples get more defined and stand up straight. During this phase, the male urethral sphincter contracts (to keep urine from mixing with semen and to safeguard against retrograde ejaculation), and muscles at the base of the penis begin a continuous cadenced contraction. Both of these actions are intended to keep urine from mixing with semen and to guard against retrograde ejaculation. The gonads of males may start to ascend nearer to the body, at which point they may begin to leak seminal liquid or pre-ejaculatory liquid. With regards to females, the plateau stage is fundamentally a continuation of the alterations that were seen during the enthusiasm time frame. The clitoris turns out to be incredibly delicate and pulls back a tiny bit of spot, while at the same time, the Bartholin glands create more lubricant. The muscles of the pubococcygeus fix, and the tissues of the external third of the vagina enlarge, which together outcome in a decrease in the diameter of the entrance of the vagina. Orgasmic platform is what Masters and Johnson allude to when they talk about the changes that take place all through the plateau stage. This is the pinnacle of sexual ecstasy for individuals who have always been unable to reach orgasm.

- **Orgasm**: A series of contractions, which may number anywhere from 1 to 20 or more in the sequence, take place in the pelvis of the female during the process of giving birth. These contractions occur every 8/10ths of a second. The anal and urinary sphincter muscles, as well as the smooth muscles in the inner segment of the vagina, as well as the puboccocceygeus muscles, are all involved in the contractions. Additionally, an electrical feeling surges from the clitoris and radiates all through the body. This activates the pleasure areas of the brain as well as the development of the hormone known as oxytocin, sometimes known as the "boding hormone." When the orgasm is finished, the body ultimately returns to the condition it was in before it was energized. In general, in comparison to men, females are able to go through labor with a greater number of contractions spread out over a more extended timeframe. It has been shown that females have a far greater capability for sexual interaction than men do. This indicates that females are able to have more sexual experiences, on a more regular basis, and with additional orgasms than the typical person is capable of.

The plateau phase of the sexual reaction cycle is separated by the sensation of orgasm, which is shared by the two men and females. At the point when an individual is having an orgasmic experience, the muscles in their lower pelvis, which encompass both the anus and the major sexual organs, go through rapid patterns of muscular contraction. Orgasms are often accompanied by a variety of additional involuntary behaviors, like vocalizations, muscle spasms in different parts of the body, and a generally euphoric feeling. The pace of the heartbeat accelerates considerably more.

Tantric sexual practices could have the target of reducing the importance of obtaining orgasm, which is often one of the most prevalent goals of sexual experiences.

Ejaculation is often capable simultaneously with orgasm in folks. Each discharge is trailed by continual beats of sexual pleasure, particularly in the penis and the areas immediately around it. A strong feeling of something else may be felt among the lower spine or the lower back. In many cases, the first and second spasms are the most impressive with regards to feeling and result in the creation of the greatest amount of semen. After then, at that point, each contraction is associated with a decreased volume of semen and a mellower feeling of pleasure. This continues until the climax of the interaction.

Uterine and vaginal contractions are also something that ladies feel. Orgasms in females could look very changed depending on the individual experiencing them. It is general information that they bring about an increase in vaginal lubrication, a snugness of the vaginal walls, and an overall pleasant sensation. There is also the chance of female ejaculation, which is ordinarily alluded to as "squirting." this may happen to certain ladies.

It has been shown that females have a far greater capability for sexual interaction than men do. This indicates that females are able to have more sexual experiences, more regularly, and with additional orgasms than the typical person is capable of.

The Sexual Experience

Regardless of whether the physiological aspect of sexuality is shared across the genders, it is possible that the physical longings that people have for sexual activity are not the same. Studies reveal that ladies' sexual longing is more delicate to the specific circumstance (meaningful or personal association) and the social and cultural climate (quality of relationships, stressors of the day, etc.). This has been shown endlessly time again. Given the possible "cost" to a woman throughout the span of her lifetime of having sexual experiences, this shouldn't shock anyone. A female doesn't have the biological extravagance of being able to walk away from a sexual experience without running the gamble of becoming pregnant or having to raise a youngster, whereas a man always has the chance of doing so.

The method wherein individuals have sexual encounters and communicate their thoughts sexually is alluded to as human sexuality. This encompasses sensations and actions that are biological, psychological, physical, sexual, emotional, social, or spiritual in nature. It is hard to define unequivocally because such a wide idea its meaning has changed over the span of history in light of changing circumstances. The human reproductive activities, including the human sexual reaction cycle, are primarily the focal point of the biological and physical parts of sexuality. Sexuality is also defined by the human body's reaction to sexual stimulation.

The pattern of an individual's sexual interest, whether it be in the opposing sex or the same sex, may give insight into that individual's sexual orientation. The emotional and physical parts of sexuality involve the formation of relationships between people, which may be communicated via intense feelings or the outward demonstrations of adoration, trust, and caring. Spirituality is worried about an individual's spiritual association with others, while the social elements of sexuality deal with the influence that human society has on an individual's sexuality. The cultural, political, legal, intellectual, moral, ethical, and strict elements of life all have an impact on sexuality, and sexuality in turn has an impact on these aspects.

When a person approaches puberty, they often have a greater interest in engaging in sexual behavior. Even while no one hypothesis on the reasons of sexual orientation has yet acquired universal acceptance, there is a great deal more evidence supporting nonsocial causes of sexual orientation than social ones, particularly for men. This is especially true when comparing the evidence for social and nonsocial causes of sexual orientation. The social explanations that have been hypothesized are only supported by flimsy evidence, which has been skewed by a large number of confounding variables. This is further corroborated by research gathered from other cultures, which show that societies that are accepting of homosexuality do not have considerably greater rates of homosexuality among their populations. Additional viewpoints on sexuality may be gained from an evolutionary perspective on human partnering, reproduction, and reproductive strategies, as well as from the social learning theory. Aspects of sexuality that are part of the sociocultural context include historical changes and religious beliefs. It's been said that some societies are more restrictive when it comes to sexual behavior. The study of sexuality also encompasses human identity within the context of social groupings, birth control techniques, as well as sexually transmitted diseases and illnesses (STDs/STIs).

5.4 FEMALE ANATOMICAL AND PHYSIOLOGICAL DYSFUNCTION

- **Pelvic Inflammatory Disease (PID)**

The open-ended shape of the uterine tubes may have major adverse effects on a person's health in the event that bacteria or other infectious agents enter the body via the vagina, travel through the uterus, and then enter the tubes before entering the pelvic cavity. In the event that this is not addressed, a bacterial infection, often known as sepsis, may rapidly become life-threatening. When abortions are carried out by inexperienced medical professionals in settings that are not sterile, there is a heightened risk of the infection spreading in this way. In addition, sepsis has been linked to sexually transmitted bacterial diseases, including gonorrhea and chlamydia. These factors make a woman bound to foster pelvic inflammatory disease (PID), an infection that may affect the uterine cylinders or any of the other reproductive organs. PID may leave scar tissue in the cylinders, which can lead to infertility even after the condition has been treated.

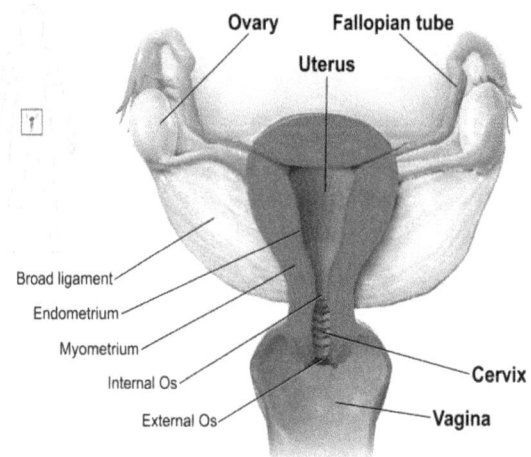

Figure 5.6: Pelvic Inflammatory Disease

In addition, sepsis has been linked to sexually transmit bacterial diseases, including gonorrhea and chlamydia. These factors make a woman bound to foster pelvic inflammatory disease (PID), an infection that may affect the uterine cylinders or any of the other reproductive organs. PID may leave scar tissue in the cylinders, which can lead to infertility even after the condition has been treated.

Bacteria may travel from the vaginal canal to the cervix, which is how the illness is contracted. In spite of the fact that it has been documented that infections by Neisseria gonorrhoeae or Chlamydia trachomatis are present in 75 to 90 percent of patients, the significant link of PID with these diseases is frequently a mistake. It has been reported by the National Health Service (NHS) in the United Kingdom that infections caused by Neisseria gonorrhoeae and Chlamydia trachomatis account for barely a quarter of PID cases. It is not uncommon for more than one kind of bacterium to be involved.

In the absence of therapy, PID will develop in around 10 percent of individuals who have a chlamydial infection and in approximately 40 percent of those who have a gonorrhea infection. A large number of sexual partners and substance abuse are two of the risk variables, which are typically comparable to those associated with sexually transmitted infections (STIs). Douching the vaginal area with liquid may also raise the risk. In most cases, the diagnosis is determined by looking at the patient's current signs and symptoms. It is suggested that the condition be considered in all women of reproductive age who are experiencing lower abdomen discomfort. This is because the disease might cause complications during pregnancy. During surgery, if pus is found to be affecting the fallopian tubes, a PID diagnosis may be confirmed with 100 percent certainty. In addition, ultrasound might be helpful in the diagnostic process.

One way to avoid contracting the illness is to abstain from sexual activity, limit the number of partners one has in a sexual relationship, and always use a condom. PID risk may be reduced by screening high-risk women for chlamydial infection and then treating those who test positive for the illness. Treatment is normally recommended if there is even a remote possibility that a diagnosis may be present. In addition to treating a lady, her sexual partners need to be cared for. It is advised that patients who are exhibiting only mild or moderate symptoms have a single injection of the antibiotic ceftriaxone, in addition to taking doxycycline orally for two weeks and potentially metronidazole as well. Antibiotics administered intravenously should be used for patients who show no signs of improvement after three days or who have a severe condition.

In the year 2008, there were about 106 million cases of chlamydia and 106 million cases of gonorrhea announced over the world. In any case, it is obscure the number of individuals that have been affected by PID. It is accepted that around 1.5 percent of young ladies are affected by it each year. It is predicted that each year around one million persons in the United States may suffer with PID. During the 1970s, there was an increase in the prevalence of preterm birth due to the use of an intrauterine device (IUD) called the Dalkon shield. After the first month of use, none of the currently available IUDs are linked to this issue.

- **Endometriosis**

Endometriosis is a condition where endometrial cells implant and foster in locations other than the uterus, like the uterine cylinders, the ovaries, or even the pelvic cavity itself. This may cause extreme pain and different side effects. Endometriosis is characterized by the development of tissue beyond the uterus that is anatomically comparable to the tissue that lines the uterus. This tissue will tear apart and leak at the finish of the cycle, much as normal uterine tissue does when you are having your period. However, there is no place for this blood to go. It's possible that the districts around it may balloon or foster inflammation. You could have scar tissue and injuries. The ovaries are the most typical location for endometriosis to manifest itself.

Endometriosis is a condition where tissue that is analogous to the lining of the uterus creates in places other than the actual uterus. It may also make it harder to imagine a youngster as well as create acute distress in the pelvic.

Endometriosis may begin with an individual's absolute first menstruation and continue all the way until menopause for certain ladies. Endometriosis is a condition wherein tissue that is analogous to the uterine lining creates beyond the uterus. This outcomes in inflammation and the formation of scar tissue in the pelvic area, as well as (sometimes) in different parts of the body. There is no great reason for what causes endometriosis. Endometriosis is as of now preventable in no known method at this time. Although there is no known fix, the side effects may be managed with medication and, in rare circumstances, surgical intervention. It creates a drawn out inflammatory reaction, which may lead to the improvement of scar tissue (adhesions, fibrosis) inside the pelvis and perhaps in different areas of the body. Several distinct types of injuries have been accounted for, including:

- **Yeast Infection (Vaginal Candidiasis)**

A yeast infection is a fungal infection that may irritate the vulva and produce discharge from the vagina. Yeast infections are very normal. Yeast infections are very prevalent in females, affecting generally 75% of ladies sooner or later in their lives. Fortunately, treatment for yeast infections is easy. A yeast infection of the vagina is a fungal infection that causes irritation, discharge, and acute itching of the vagina and the vulva, which are the tissues near the vaginal entrance. Yeast infections are the most well-known kind of vaginal infections.

A vaginal yeast infection, which is also known as vaginal candidiasis, may afflict as many as three out of every four women at some point in their lives. A significant number of women have at least two episodes. it is not regarded to be a sexually transmitted infection if a yeast infection occurs in the vaginal area. However, during the time of one's first regular sexual activity, the chance of developing a vaginal yeast infection is significantly enhanced. There is also some evidence that mouth-to-genital contact, often known as oral-genital sex, may be associated to the spread of illnesses. Medications are a viable option for treating vaginal yeast infections efficiently. It is possible that you may need a more extensive treatment course as well as a maintenance plan if you have recurrent yeast infections, which are defined as four or more instances within a single year.

The overgrowth of yeast in the vagina, which may also be referred to as vaginal thrush and candidal vulvovaginitis, can lead to discomfort. This condition is known as a vaginal yeast infection. Itching in the vaginal region is the most prevalent symptom, and it may be very severe. Additional symptoms include a burning sensation while urination, a thick, white vaginal discharge that does not normally smell unpleasant, discomfort experienced during sexual activity, and redness around the vagina. Symptoms often get more severe in the days leading up to a woman's menstruation. Yeast infections in the vaginal tract are brought on by an overgrowth of Candida. In a healthy vaginal environment, only trace amounts of these yeasts will be found. Candida albicans is the type of yeast that is most often responsible for vaginal yeast infections. Candida albicans is a common fungus that may often be found living in a person's mouth, digestive system, or vagina even in the absence of any indications of illness. Although the characteristics that predispose someone to have excessive Candida development have been discovered, the reasons of excessive Candida growth are not fully understood. Although it is not considered a sexually transmitted illness, those who engage in regular sexual activity may be more likely to get the condition than those who do not. The use of antibiotics, pregnancy, diabetes, and HIV/AIDS are all considered to be risk factors. It does not apparent that characteristics such as wearing tight clothes, having a certain brand of underwear, or having poor personal hygiene are contributors. The diagnosis is made by conducting tests on a sample of the patient's vaginal discharge. Because the symptoms are comparable to those of sexually transmitted diseases including chlamydia and gonorrhea, testing could be suggested.

Antifungal medicine is used in the treatment of the condition. This treatment may be administered topically, using a cream like clotrimazole, or orally, using drugs like fluconazole. Despite the absence of proof, cotton underwear and clothing that is loose fitting are often advised as preventative measures. It is suggested that you also refrain from douching and using perfumed personal care products It has been discovered that probiotics are not helpful in treating active illnesses. At some time in their life, around 75% of women will get at least one vaginal yeast infection, and almost half of all women will experience at least two infections. Roughly five percent of people will get more than three illnesses in a single year. After bacterial vaginosis, it is the second most prevalent cause of vaginal irritation. Bacterial vaginosis is the most common cause.

- **PMS**

Between ovulation and the start of a period, a collection of symptoms known as premenstrual syndrome may make a woman feel both physically and emotionally unwell. The severity of the symptoms might range from being hardly noticeable in some women to being incapacitating in others. The disruptive mental and physical symptoms known as premenstrual syndrome (PMS) often occur in the week or two before the onset of a woman's menstrual cycle. When menstruation starts, symptoms usually disappear. Women's symptoms vary greatly from one another. Symptoms of premenstrual syndrome might include changes in physical health, mental state, or behavior, and typically subside once menstruation begins. Common symptoms include breast soreness, bloating, headache, mood swings, melancholy, anxiety, rage, and irritability, although there is a broad spectrum of discomforts that may be experienced. Two consecutive menstrual cycles of symptom disruption are required for a diagnosis of premenstrual syndrome rather than just regular period pain. These symptoms are not exclusive to women experiencing premenstrual syndrome. The average duration of PMS-related symptoms is six days. The symptom patterns a person experience may change over time. Neither pregnancy nor menopause causes PMS symptoms. For a diagnosis to be made, there must be a pattern of disruptive mental and physical symptoms that occur after ovulation and before menstruation. The beginning of a woman's menstrual cycle should not be accompanied by any emotional symptoms. Keeping track of your symptoms on a daily basis for a few months might aid in diagnosis. The diagnosis can only be established when all other possible causes of the symptoms have been ruled out. It is unclear what triggers premenstrual syndrome (PMS), however it is thought that fluctuating hormone levels throughout the menstrual cycle have a role. In moderate cases, reducing sodium, alcohol, caffeine, and stress and increasing physical activity are all that is suggested. Some people may benefit from taking a calcium and vitamin D supplement. Physical symptoms may be alleviated by taking an anti-inflammatory medication such ibuprofen or naproxen. Birth control medications and the diuretic spironolactone may help people with more severe symptoms.

Premenstrual symptoms, such as bloating, headaches, and moodiness, are experienced by more than 90% of women. Only around 20% of premenopausal women experience PMS-level disturbance from their premenstrual symptoms. The emotional side effects of premenstrual syndrome (PMS) may be treated with antidepressants belonging to the particular serotonin reuptake inhibitor (SSRI) family. More serious psychological side effects are seen in premenstrual dysphoric problem (PMDD). About 3% of reproductive-age ladies experience the ill effects of premenstrual dysphoric issue (PMDD).

PCOS/Ovarian cysts

Fluid-filled sacs that may be seen in or on an ovary are referred to as ovarian cysts. Polycystic ovarian syndrome, often known as PCOS, is a hormonal condition that may lead to the development of many cysts on the ovaries, which may (or may not) have an effect on ovulation. Women who have PCOS might have irregular or unusually broadened menstrual cycles, as well as elevated amounts of male hormones.

- **Fibroid tumors**

Fibroids are abnormal developments that may shape in or on the muscular wall of a woman's uterus. They can be painful and can cause infertility. These growths have the potential to turn out to be exceptionally huge and cause distress in the abdomen locale as well as infertility. Fibroids of the uterus are harmless developments of the uterus that most frequently manifest themselves during a woman's reproductive years. Uterine fibroids, which are also known as leiomyomas (lie-o-my-O-muhs) or myomas, are not linked to an elevated gamble of uterine cancer and usually never progress into malignancy. Fibroids may vary in size from seedlings that are excessively little to be seen by the naked eye to huge masses that can cause the uterus to become misshapen and enlarged. At least one fibroids may be available in your body at the same time. In serious situations, the presence of many fibroids may cause the uterus to enlarge to the point where it pushes facing the rib cage, which can bring about an increase in body weight.

Uterine fibroids are a typical condition that affects many women eventually in their life. Nonetheless, since uterine fibroids often produce no side effects, it is possible that you are unaware that you have them. During a pelvic check or a pregnancy ultrasound, your physician can happen upon the presence of fibroids by accident.

5.5 BREASTS

The breast is made up of many different types of tissue: glandular, ductal, connective, and adipose. Fat and lobules are what make up the mammary glands, and they are found embedded in the fibrous tissue. Mammary glands are important for reproduction in women, but they are rudimentary and nonfunctional in males. The breasts of males typically contain very little fat, and the glandular system does not develop at all. The quantity of fat that is put away in the glandular tissue is what defines the size of a woman's breasts since the breasts are the most noticeable superficial design located on the anterior thoracic wall. It is normal for a tiny part of the mammary gland to stretch out into the axilla, where it structures what is known as the axillary tail of Spence.

Despite the fact that they are separated from the rest of the female reproductive organs by a significant distance, breasts are nevertheless regarded to be part of the female reproductive system. Lactation is the process through which a newborn receives milk from his or her mother via the use of the breasts. The nipple of the breast is encircled by a pigmented areola, the pigmentation of which might become more profound during pregnancy. This is one of the outward characteristics of the breast. The areola is normally round in shape, and its diameter may range anywhere from 25 to 100 millimeters (mm). During breastfeeding, the areolar area produces a lubricating fluid that prevents the nipple from being chafed. These areolar glands are tiny and elevated and have a characteristic appearance. When a newborn nurses, also known as sucking milk from a breast, the whole area around the areolar glands is brought into the mouth.

Mammary glands, which are essentially altered sweat glands, are liable for the creation of breast milk. There are anywhere from 15 to 20 lactiferous pipes that open on the surface of the areola, and these are the passageways via which the actual milk is ousted from the breast. These lactiferous channels each stretch out to a lactiferous sinus, which links to a glandular curve inside the actual breast. The glandular curve includes gatherings of milk-secreting cells in bunches called alveoli. Each of these lactiferous channels reaches out to a lactiferous sinus. The quantity of milk that is available in the alveolar lumen has an impact on the size of the bunches that are delivered. Whenever milk has been created in the alveoli, activated myoepithelial cells that encompass the alveoli will contract in request to move the milk to the lactiferous sinuses. Suckling allows the infant to access the lactiferous pipes, which allow it to take milk from the mother's breast. The actual curves are encased in a layer of fatty tissue, which is what defines the overall size of the breast. The size of a woman's breasts varies from one individual to another and has no impact on the quantity of milk that she delivers. Numerous bands of connective tissue known as suspensory ligaments link the breast tissue to the dermis of the skin that covers the breasts. These ligaments offer help for the breasts.

Mammary glands are sweat glands that have been changed to produce milk. Mammary glands consist of 15-20 lobules, each of which is emptied by a lactiferous duct. Each lactiferous duct has its own separate drainage on the nipple, and they are preceded by a little dilated area that is referred to as the lactiferous sinus. The nipple in the middle of the breasts is surrounded by pigmented areola, which darkens during pregnancy. Milk gathers in the sinus during feeding and is "let down" by the sucking movement of the newborn. The process of lactation is termed "letting down." Each breast has anything from 10 to 20 lobes, and each lobe has anywhere from 20 to 40 lobules, and each lobule has anywhere from 20 to 80 alveoli.

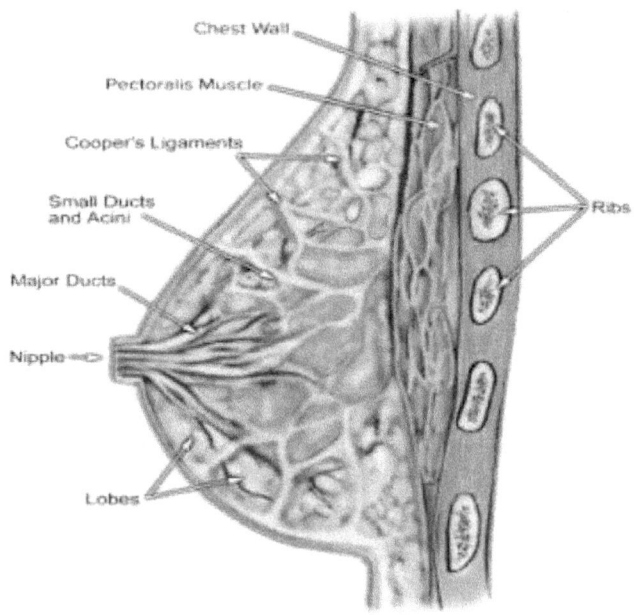

Figure 5.7: Female breast

After the placenta is removed, there is an unexpected change in the degrees of estrogen and progesterone in the body. This is because, all through pregnancy, the placenta creates high quantities of estrogen and progesterone, the two of which cutoff milk creation. At the point when an infant breastfeeds, this triggers the creation of a hormone called prolactin from the pituitary gland located somewhere inside the brain. Sucking by an infant induces the development of milk as well as stimulates the release of the hormone oxytocin from the back pituitary gland. This allows the milk to be ousted from the alveoli and into the ductal framework. Prolactin is answerable for this. The quantity of fatty tissue present in the breasts is straightforwardly proportional to the size of the breasts.

The breast is one of two prominences that are placed on the top ventral part of a primate's middle, and it is the larger of the two. Breasts may frame in the two men and females since they develop from the same tissues in the embryo.

In females, it carries out the role of the mammary gland, which is liable for the creation and secretion of milk to support youthful. A network of channels that unite on the areola are covered and encased by subcutaneous fat, and these tissues are liable for giving the breast its size and structure. Milk is created and put away in the lobules, also known as bunches of alveoli, at the closures of the conduits. These lobules answer hormonal signals by producing milk. The breast reacts all through pregnancy to a perplexing combination of hormones, including estrogens, progesterone, and prolactin, which regulate the completion of its turn of events, namely lobuloalveolar maturation, in preparation for lactation and nursing. Over the course of this time, the lobuloalveolar maturation process takes place. Just humans, alone among animals, have breasts that don't fall off. In female humans, the permanent advancement of breast tissue is welcomed on during pubescence by the interaction of estrogens and development hormone. This is the kind of thing that just happens to a lot smaller amount in different primates, and breast development in different primates often just takes place during pregnancy. In addition to their primary reason, which is to give sustenance to kids, the social and sexual features of female breasts are also present. Breasts have appeared in sculptural works, paintings, and photographs from both ancient and contemporary times. They have the potential to have a significant job in how the physical make-up and sexual attractiveness of a woman are seen. Breasts are associated with sexuality in various societies, and individuals from these societies often consider it discourteous or vulgar to uncover their breasts out in the open. Erogenous zones may be tracked down in the breasts, particularly the areolas.

Breast tissue reacts to varying degrees of estrogen and progesterone during the typical hormonal variations that happen all through the menstrual cycle. This reaction may cause certain individuals to encounter swelling and breast uneasiness, particularly during the secretory phase of the cycle. On the off chance that pregnancy happens, the ascent in hormone levels causes further development of the mammary tissue, which brings about an increase in the size of the breasts.

- **Hormonal Birth Control**

To forestall pregnancy and inhibit ovulation, contraception pills make utilization of a negative feedback mechanism that controls the ovarian and menstrual cycles. This framework is liable for keeping women from becoming pregnant. In many cases, they capability by maintaining a steady degree of both estrogen and progesterone in the body. This has the impact of exerting a negative feedback circle on the hypothalamus and pituitary, which stops the creation of FSH and LH. If there is not enough FSH, the follicles will not develop, and ovulation will not take place if there is not enough LH surge. Even though birth control tablets include estrogen, which does encourage some thickening of the endometrial wall, this thickening is not as significant as it would be during a regular cycle, and hence implantation is less likely to occur.

There are seven inactive pills (placebos) and 21 hormone-containing active tablets that are included inside some types of birth control pills. The decrease in hormones that happens while the woman is taking the placebo tablets causes menstruation to begin, yet the stream is often lighter than a normal menstrual stream since the endometrium has not had as much chance to solidify as it would have in any case. they fresher varieties of conception prevention tablets supply a low dosage of estrogens and progesterone all through the entire cycle (they should be utilized 365 days out of the year), and menstruation never takes place. Menstruation like clockwork isn't necessary for health reasons, and there are no recorded sick results of not having a menstrual period a generally healthy. in an individual. Notwithstanding, there are a few women who like to have the proof of a lack of pregnancy that a month to month time span gives. This proof may be obtained by having a period.

In any event, missing only a couple of conception prevention pills at certain points in the menstrual cycle (or in any event, taking the pill several hours late) can bring about an increase in follicle-stimulating hormone (FSH) and luteinizing hormone (LH), the two of which can lead to ovulation. This is because contraception pills capability by providing constant estrogen and progesterone levels and disrupting negative feedback. In this way, in request for the woman to successfully avoid pregnancy, it is essential that she adhere to the instructions that are printed on the packaging of the anti-conception medication pill.

5.5.1 Anatomy

At women, the pectoralis major muscles are covered by the breasts, and the breasts stretch on average from the level of the second rib to the level of the 6th rib at the front of the rib cage. Thus, the breasts cover a significant piece of the chest district and the chest walls. In the front of the chest, the breast tissue may reach all the way to the focal point of the sternum (breastbone), which is located just underneath the clavicle (collarbone). The breast tissue may stretch out into the axilla (armpit) along the edges of the chest, and it can reach as far back as the latissimus dorsi muscle, which runs from the lower back to the humerus bone (the bone of the upper arm) in the back. The breast, which is a mammary gland, is made up of several layers of tissue, the majority of which are of two distinct sorts: adipose tissue and glandular tissue, the latter of which influences the activities of the breasts related to breastfeeding.

The breast has the type of a teardrop according to a morphological viewpoint. Between 0.5 to 2.5 centimeters of subcutaneous fat (adipose tissue) sits between the skin and the superficial tissue layer, also known as the superficial fascia. The strained anticipation Cooper's ligaments are sinewy tissue prolongations that stretch out from the superficial fascia to the skin envelope. They are named after the physician who found them. There are anywhere from 14 to 18 irregular lactiferous curves in an adult female breast, all of which meet up at the areola. The solid connective tissue that upholds the glands is immediately around the milk channels that range in size from 2.0 to 4.5 millimeters. The areola is a pigmented locale of skin that encompasses the areola, which is the opening through which milk is ousted from the breast. The size of the areola may vary greatly starting with one woman then onto the next. Montgomery's glands may be seen inside the areola. These glands have been adjusted to create sweat. During nursing, these glands will generate a sleek liquid that will both lubricate and safeguard the areola. The volatile atoms that are included within these secretions have the potential to work as an olfactory stimulant for the yearning of the baby.

The size of a woman's breast as well as its weight may vary greatly starting with one woman then onto the next. The average load of a small to medium-sized breast is under 1.1 pounds (500 grams), whereas the average load of a major breast is between 750 and 1,000 grams (1.7 to 2.2 pounds) or more. Epithelial or glandular tissue just accounts for around 10 to 20 percent of the volume of the breasts, while stromal tissue, which includes fat and connective tissue, makes up about 80 to 90 percent of the breasts. The breasts are made up of about 80 to 90 percent stromal tissue (fat and connective tissue). Additionally, the breast tissue structure ratios vary starting with one woman then onto the next. In the breasts of certain women, the percentage of glandular tissue is a lot greater compared to the percentages of adipose tissue and connective tissue. The extent of connective tissue to fatty tissue is a vital factor in determining the thickness of the breasts. Because of fluctuations in hormone levels that happen all through pubescence, the menstrual cycle, pregnancy, lactation, and menopause, a woman's breasts will alter in size, shape, and weight all through her lifetime.

Anatomy is the area of science that is worried about the investigation of the construction of organisms and their parts. "Anatomy" comes from the Ancient Greek word "o" (anatom), and that means "analyzation." The investigation of anatomy is a sub-discipline within the natural sciences that spotlights on the organizational designs of living organisms. This is an extremely ancient field of study, with its foundations going back to ancient times. Because these are the mechanisms by which anatomy is shaped, both across immediate and long haul timeframes, anatomy is naturally related to developmental science, embryology, comparative anatomy, evolutionary science, and phylogeny. This is because developmental science, embryology, comparative anatomy, evolutionary science, and phylogeny are all subfields of evolutionary science. Anatomy and physiology, the relative investigations of the construction and capability of organisms and their parts, contain a natural pair of linked sciences, and are often concentrated together because of the cozy relationship between the two. One of the fundamental logical disciplines that are indispensable to the practice of medicine is human anatomy.

The investigation of anatomy is an intricate and dynamic discipline that is always developing because of new disclosures being made. Lately, there has been a substantial development in the usage of sophisticated imaging methods, including as MRI and CT scans, which give more exact and accurate representations of the designs inside the body. Examples of these imaging strategies are magnetic resonance imaging (MRI) and figured tomography (CT).

The investigation of anatomy may be separated into two categories: macroscopic and minute. The inspection of an animal's substantial parts using simply the vision that they were brought into the world with is known as macroscopic anatomy or gross anatomy. The subfield of superficial anatomy is included within the umbrella of gross anatomy. Histology, which is another name for the investigation of the tissues of different designs, and the investigation of cells, both fall under the umbrella of infinitesimal anatomy. Infinitesimal anatomy requires the utilization of optical instruments.

The improvement of a more profound information on the jobs played by the many organs and designs of the human body may be viewed as a unifying subject over the course of anatomy. The inspection of animals used to include the analyzation of animal carcasses and cadavers (bodies). Nonetheless, in the twentieth 100 years, medical imaging methods like X-ray, ultrasound, and magnetic resonance imaging were created, which addressed a significant improvement over the past method.

- **Glandular structure**

Apocrine glands, similar to those tracked down in the breast, are liable for the creation of milk, which is used to take care of an infant. The maxim "areola complex" alludes to the area of the breast that contains both the areola and the areola. There are a lot of sebaceous glands in the areola, and the shade of the skin may range from pink to dark brown. The terminal course lobular units (TDLUs), which are liable for the creation of the fatty breast milk, are the fundamental units that make up the breast. Mammary glands are liable for the activities of the breast that are related to the feeding of young. They are scattered over the whole of the breast's physical development. Within a distance of thirty millimeters of the lower part of the areola, about 66% of the lactiferous tissue may be found. The milk is drained from the terminal lactiferous channels, which are located in the TDLUs, into 4-18 lactiferous pipes, which then, at that point, drain into the areola. In a nursing woman, the ratio of milk glands to fat is, a not lactating, the 2:1, but in a woman isn't lactating, the ratio is 1:1. In addition to the milk glands, the breast is made up of connective tissues (collagen and elastin), white fat, and the Cooper's ligaments, which act as a suspension framework. The innervation of the breast is carried out by the peripheral tactile framework through the front (anterior) and side (lateral) cutaneous branches of the fourth, fifth, and sixth intercostal nerves. These nerves are answerable for providing the sensation felt in the breast. The areola complex accepts its feeling from the T-4 nerve, which is the fourth thoracic spinal nerve. This nerve also innervates the dermatomic area.

- **Lymphatic drainage**

It is estimated that around 75% of the lymph that drains from the breast makes its way to the axillary lymph center points located on the same side of the body, while the remaining 25% of the lymph makes its way to the parasternal center points located adjacent to the sternum bone. A trace quantity of lymph that is abandoned streams to the contrary breast as well as the lymph centers in the abdominal cavity. A lymphatic plexus that is located in the subareolar area is alluded to as the "subareolar plexus of Sappey." The pectoral (chest), subscapular (under the scapula), and humeral (humerus-bone locale) lymph-center packs are all included in the axillary lymph center points. These lymph-center packs eventually drain into the central axillary lymph center points as well as the apical axillary lymph centers. Because breast cancer is so prevalent in the mammary gland and cancer cells may metastasis (break out) from a development and be circulated to various areas of the body through the lymphatic framework, the lymphatic drainage of the breasts is of particular relevance to the area of oncology.

- **Shape, texture, and support**

The natural structure, pectoral location, and spacing of a woman's breasts, as well as how they appear and feel, are all determined by the morphologic contrasts that exist in their size, shape, volume, tissue thickness, pectoral localization, and spacing. There is no correlation between the size of a woman's breasts and the ratio of fat to drain glands in her breast tissue or the ability of the mother to breastfeed an infant. Both the size and the type of the breasts may be affected by hormonal movements that happen naturally during an individual's lifetime (for example, during pubescence, menstruation, pregnancy, and menopause) as well as by medical diseases, (for example, virginal breast hypertrophy). The help of the suspensory Cooper's ligaments, the underlying muscle and bone designs of the chest, and the skin envelope all work together to establish the type of the breasts organically. By traveling through and surrounding the tissues of the breast's fat and milk glands, the suspensory ligaments keep the breast attached to the clavicle (collarbone) and the clavico-pectoral fascia (which associates the collarbone to the chest). The skin envelope is answerable for giving the breast its structure and ensuring that it retains that shape over the course of time. The breast is situated, attached, and upheld by the chest wall. One breast will in general be somewhat greater than the other in the majority of women. Asymmetry of the breasts that is both more noticeable and more persevering may happen in as many as 25% of women. Researchers have determined that a woman's breasts sag owing to four important factors: cigarette smoking, number of pregnancies, gravity, and weight reduction or gain. Regardless of the fact that a prevalent assumption nursing causes breasts to sag, researchers have demonstrated that this isn't the case.

The profound fascia that lies over the pectoralis major muscles is answerable for attaching the lower part of each breast to the chest. The breast can move because of an area known as the retromammary space, which is located between the chest wall and the pectoralis major muscle. From the thoracic inlet (which is located on top of the breastbone) and upwards to the least ribs that help the breasts, the chest (thoracic cavity) gradually slants outwards in an outward course. The inframammary overlay, also known as the IMF or the least most expansion of the anatomic breast, is a feature that is generated anatomically when the breast skin adheres to the underlying connective tissues of the chest. This feature may be seen at the point where the lower part of the breast meets the chest. The surface of normal breast tissue is often depicted as feeling nodular or granular, yet how much this is the case may vary a seriously little starting with one woman then onto the next.

5.6 PELVIS

The pelvis is a structure that has the form of a basin and serves to both support the spinal column and shield the abdominal organs. The following are included in it: Sacrum. A bone with the shape of a spade that is generated by the union of five sacral vertebrae that were previously distinct. The coccyx is often referred to as the tail bone.

The region of the female abdominal cavity that extends downward and is situated between the hip bones. In general, the female pelvis is more delicate than the male pelvis, which is also broader than it is and not as high as it is. The female pubic arch has a circular and broad angle at its point of origin. The sacrum of a female is more expansive than that of a man, whereas the iliac bone in the female is more concave. When compared to that of a man, the pelvic basin of a female has greater room and is less channel shaped overall. When compared to the pelvis of a man, the pelvis of a woman is better able to accept a growing fetus during the course of pregnancy and to make space for the conveyance of the baby at the finish of the pregnancy.

Symptoms of a pelvic condition

The following is a list of common symptoms that may be caused by a pelvic condition:

- a dull ache or discomfort in the pelvic and lower abdomen
- a sensation in the pelvis that may be described as either pressure or fullness
- strange or foul-smelling vaginal discharge
- a painful experience during sexual activity bleeding in between periods
- cramping that is unpleasant and occurs during or before periods

- a painful sensation while peeing or having bowel motions and a scalding sensation when urinating

5.6.1 The composition of hip bone

The ilium, pubis, and ischium are the three components that come together to form the hip bone. The ilium, which is the broadest and longest of the three components, contributes to the formation of the uppermost portion of the hip bone. The pubis is the part of the hip bone that is located farthest front. The ischium is responsible for forming the posterior-inferior portion of the hip bone. The pelvic cavity is separated into two sections: the false pelvic and the genuine pelvic. The top portion of the pelvis is called the false pelvic, and it is formed by the two ilia. Important markers and the point at which the distance between the ischium and the pelvic cavity is at its shortest are the ischial spines, which are strong projections that define the posterior border of the ischium. The actual pelvis, which includes the pelvic cavity, the inlet, and the outflow, is of the utmost significance throughout the birthing process.

The hip bones, also known as the pelvic bones or the coxal bones, are large irregular bones that are a component of the pelvic girdle. Other names for these bones include the sacrum and the ilium. When seen from the front, the two hip bones are connected by the pubic symphysis, which is a secondary cartilaginous joint. When viewed from the back, however, they interact with the sacrum via the sacroiliac joints, which are synovial joints. Due to the fact that they are a component of the pelvic girdle, they assist in the movement of weight from the upper body to the lower limbs.

Each individual hip bone is composed of three distinct subparts, which are labeled as follows: 1) the ilium (located superiorly), 2) the ischium (located posterior inferiorly), and 3) the pubis (located anterioroinferiorly). The acetabulum, which is a hollow region in the shape of a cup and is located on the outside of the hip bone, is where the three parts come together to form the whole. A big oval aperture that is known as the obturator foramen is located inferiorly, and it is what separates the pubis and the ischium from one another.

- **Ilium** - The ilium is the highest and most developed portion of the hip bone. On the medial surface of the ilium, there is a rounded ridge that is termed the arcuate line. This ridge is a component of the linea terminalis and the pelvic brim. It does this by dividing the ilium into an upper and lower portion. A portion of the actual pelvis may be found in the lower half, which is defined as being below the pelvic brim. The top portion has the appearance of a wing-like structure that is known as the ala and is a component of the false pelvis. The iliac fossa is formed by the ala, which is concave on the inside and faces toward the gluteal area, while the outside aspect of the ala faces away from the gluteal region.

- There are three distinct advantages along the ilium. An iliac peak is framed as a thickening along the top edge, which fills in as an attachment point for various muscles. The anterior and back iliac spines, separately, act as barriers that keep it from advancing anteriorly and posteriorly. The anterior margin begins from the anterior unrivaled iliac spine and continues all the way down to the anterior inferior iliac spine. The back margin begins from the back unrivaled iliac spine and continues all the way down to the back inferior iliac spine.

- **Ischium** - The ischium is the part of the hip bone that is located on the posteroinferior aspect and includes both a major body and a ramus. The better locale of the body expands than join the ilium with the prevalent ramus of the pubis. The hamstring muscles associate with the significant ischial tuberosity that may be seen underneath it. Here the ischial tuberosity is found. A typical ischiopubic ramus is framed when the ramus of the ischium expands anteriorly and meets with the inferior ramus of the pubis.

- **Pubis** - The pubis is the portion of the hip bone that is located anterior to the inferior. It is composed of a body as well as two rami, which are referred to as superior and inferior. The body is planar and articulates with the pubic body on the opposite side to generate a secondary cartilaginous joint known as the pubic symphysis. Within the acetabular fossa, the superior ramus connects with both the ilium and the ischium, whereas the inferior ramus contributes to the formation of the ischiopubic ramus. The pectin pubis, also known as the pectineal line, is the name given to the top sharp border of the superior ramus. This area is a component of the pelvic brim.

- **Hip joint:** The hip joint is framed when the acetabulum of the hip bone and the head of the femur articulate with each other. A kind of synovial joint looks like a ball and socket and enables a broad variety of movements, like flexion, expansion, adduction, abduction, medial and lateral rotation, and circumduction.

5.6.2 Pelvic measurements

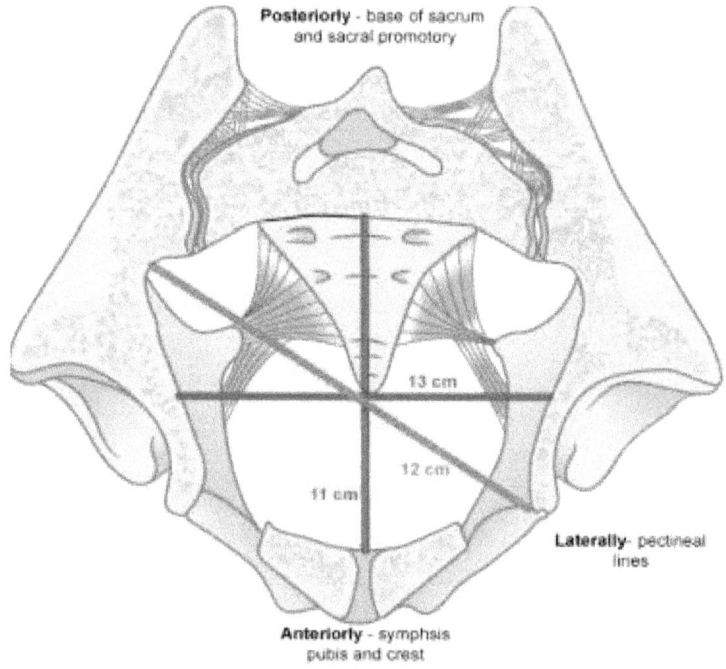

Figure 5.8: Pelvic measurements

5.6.3 Types of the pelvic

The pelvic is divided into four types:

1. **Gynaecoid (50%):** pelvic structure typical of females, which is spherical and normal.
2. **Anthropoid (20%):** which has a large opening in both the anterior and the posterior
3. **Android (20%):** male – type pelvic that has an outlet in the form of a heart
4. **Platypelloid (5%):** that has a large transverse exit and is not conducive to a vaginal birth

CHAPTER - 6

Conclusion

The female reproductive system is structured in a way that allows it to fulfill a variety of activities. It does this by producing egg cells, also known as ova, which are necessary for reproduction. The eggs will be transported to the area where they will be fertilized by the system that has been created. The Fallopian tubes are the location of the egg fertilization process, which also involves the sperm. The next step for fertilized eggs is for the embryo to attach itself to the uterine wall and begin the process that leads to a full-term pregnancy. In addition to the tasks described above, the female reproductive system is also responsible for the generation of female sexual hormones, which are necessary for the continuation of the reproductive cycle.

Ovaries, oviducts, vagina, cervix, uterus, and the external genitalia are all part of the female reproductive framework, which is situated in the pelvic area. The female reproductive framework also includes the external genitalia. The course of ovulation, fertilization, conveyance, and eventually the care of the youngster are all upheld by these parts, in addition to a pair of mammary glands that are integrated both physically and functionally.

The female reproductive framework is liable for the development of gametes (also known as eggs or ova), certain sex hormones, as well as the maintenance of treated eggs as they develop into mature fetuses and become ready for birth. The time of a woman's life that begins with menarche (the primary menstrual cycle) and finishes with menopause (the absence of menstruation for a time of a year) is alluded to as her reproductive years. Removal of ova from the ovary happens cyclically over the course of this time, and these ova have the potential to get prepared by male gametes (sperm) in the event that they are released at the ideal opportunity. The occasional release of eggs is a natural event that takes place all through a woman's menstrual cycle.

The development of the female reproductive framework includes the creation of a great number of designs, each of which is novel in their own specific manner. The primary gland is the undifferentiated gonad that later forms into the ovary in females and the testis in males. This cycle happens in the two genders. The external genetalia are the main part of the female reproductive framework that creates from the same assortment of tissues as the male designs. The remainder of the female reproductive framework develops from an altogether distinct gathering of tissues. The orchestration of this interconnected network of far-flung configurations that dwell in the brain, abdomen, pelvis, and perineum requires many explicit enzymatic proteins to coordinate the development and capability of the framework, and it requires thousands of explicit structural proteins as the actual building blocks for the framework. This network of far-flung configurations interacts with each other in request to carry out its role. The intricacy of the situation for the male is equivalent to that of the situation for the female. In this chapter, we have not even started to address the more troublesome inquiry of how these two altogether different male and female sexual frameworks created in a simultaneous way for the main male and first female of some reproductively competent species to actually mate interestingly and have all the parts fit together and capability appropriately to deliver a viable offspring. This is a troublesome inquiry because it requires an explanation of how the main male and first female of some reproductively competent species had the option to actually mate interestingly.

Internal organs of the female genital framework include the ovaries, uterine cylinders, uterus, and vagina. External organs of the female genital framework include the cervix and vulva. This framework is tracked down somewhere inside the pelvic cavity and is made up of two main parts: a glandular body known as the ovary, which is liable for the formation of oocytes and the blend of steroids; and a lengthy conduit framework, which logically adopts the names of the uterine (fallopian) tube, the uterus, and the vagina. The ovary is the glandular body of this framework. These cylinders play out a dual job by providing a course for ejaculated sperm to swim up into the peritoneal cavity and by bringing either a treated or unfertilized egg down to the uterus, where it will ultimately be removed from the body during parturition or menstruation. The uterine cylinder is an extremely straightforward cylinder that gets the oocyte from the surface of the ovary and transports it to the uterus. It is the occupation of the uterus to give a safe climate to the prepared egg to develop inside of, as well as to give sustenance to, the baby until such time as it is ready to be conveyed to the world. During labor, the vagina makes way for the baby and the placenta; yet, the vagina is also an organ of copulation and is the location where the penis and the sperm are gotten during sexual activity. The inferior vaginal canal terminates in the vulva, which is created by an assortment of organs of varied sort (dermal and erectile tissues), linking it to the beyond the body. An adnexal framework is associated with the ovary, the channels, and the vulva. This framework includes the following: In addition to the muscles, membranes, and fascia that make up the perineum, this adnexa is made up of several glands that structure around the lower end of the vagina and the urethra.

The major and auxiliary sex organs that make up the female reproductive framework are both included in this framework. Ovaries are the major sexual organs tracked down in females. In addition to producing eggs or ova, ovaries are also answerable for the secretion of female sexual hormones like progesterone and estrogen. The uterus, fallopian cylinders, cervix, and vagina are the other accessory sexual organs, along with the vagina. The clitoris, the labia minora, and the labia majora are all parts of the external genitalia. Although they are not regarded to be genital organs, the mammary glands are essential glands that are part of the female reproductive framework.

The quantity of tissues, cell types, and atoms expected for the framework to work appropriately are also multilayered. These range from skeletal muscle to smooth muscle, easy to pseudostratified to stratified epithelium, neurons and neuroendo-crine cells, many various sorts of CT cells and atoms, hormones, and neurotransmitters, and the rundown could continue endlessly. The photos, light and transmission electron micrographs, and light micrographs of these many designs are intriguing, and they give an esthetic viewpoint to the entire framework at each level. All readers interested in diving further into this fascinating subject will have their interests aroused by the tiny details that have been passed on to be shrouded in later publications.

The normal operation of the cycle female reproductive framework is much more astonishingly sophisticated than the gross and minuscule design of the organs and tissues that are involved, as was detailed in the part on physiology. This was viewed as the case while comparing the two degrees of intricacy. This intricacy starts at the zygote stage, which is when exceptionally particular qualities have to be turned on in request to begin differentiating in the preimplantation embryo. At the same time, the main part of the mRNAs that guide resulting stages of embryo, fetal, neonatal, little child, pubertal, and adult improvement have to be switched off. This is where the intricacy begins. In request to facilitate the advancement of the male fetus within the mother's belly, the DNA-determined mRNA/protein units that were essential in the beginning should be deactivated using histones, and at the same time, qualities that were already dormant should be activated. This modification would require the embryo and the baby to go through hundreds or perhaps thousands of activating and deactivating steps consistently. In addition, the improvement should contain the instructions for which cell type and what chemical union is to move to the various endpoints in the body. These instructions are expected in request for the improvement to be complete. The functional picture that has been displayed in this short summary simply scrapes the surface of all the cycles that are expected for the female side of the reproductive unit (male and female together) to operate accurately in request to generate a viable human beyond the uterus. One may be constrained to think about how humans are even capable of reproducing themselves at all. We have given a consolidated depiction of the anatomy and physiology of the typical female reproductive organization, which ought to encourage you to investigate this subject further and also give you an appreciation for the stunningly intricate plan of this very essential framework. This is because the female reproductive framework is liable for the creation of offspring.

References

1. Drake RL, Vogl AW, Mitchell AWM. Gray, Anatomía para estudiantes. 2a edn. Barcelona: Elsevier-España; 2010.
2. Albertini D, Bromfield J. Soma-germline interactions in the ovary: an evolutionary perspective. In: Verlhac M-H, Villeneuve A, editors. Oogenesis: the universal process. Chichester: Wiley-Blackwell; 2010.
3. Fertil Steril 2011; 95(7):2359-63, 2363 el. Anwar, Etin. "The Transmission of Generative Self and Women's Contribution to Conception." Gender and Self in Islam. London: Routledge, 2006. 75. Print.
4. Beier HM, Beier-Hellwig K. Molecular and cellu- lar aspects of endometrial receptivity. Hum Reprod Update. 1998; 4(5):448-58.
5. Betts, Gordon. "Anatomy and Physiology – Open Textbook." Pressbooks, 6 Mar. 2013, opentextbc.ca/anatomy and physiologyopenstax. "Models of Sexual Response." Our Bodies Ourselves, 11 Feb. 2017, www.ourbodiesourselves.org/book-excerpts/healtharticle/models-sexual-response.
6. Björndahl, L, Kvist, U. Sequence of ejaculation affects the spermatozoon as a carrier and its message. RBM Online 2003; 7:440–448.
7. Bouchet A, Cuilleret J. Anatomie topographique, descriptive et fonctionnelle. 2e edn. Villeurbanne cedex: Simep; 1982.
8. Burger H. The menopausal transition-endocrinol. ogy. J Sex Med. 2008;5(10):2266-73.
9. Burger HG, et al. A prospective longitudinal study of serum testosterone, dehydroepiandrosterone sulfate, and sex hormone-binding globulin levels through the menopause transition. J Clin Endocrinol Metab. 2000; 85(8):2832-8.
10. Burger HG, et al. The endocrinology of the meno- pausal transition: a cross-sectional study of a pop- ulation-based sample. J Clin Endocrinol Metab. 1995;80(12):3537-45.

11. Carreau, S, Bilinska, B, Levallet, J. Male germ cells. A new source of estrogens in mammalian testis. Ann. Endocrinol. 1998; 59:79–92.
12. Carrell, DT, Emery, BR, Hammoud, S. Altered protamine expression and diminished spermatogenesis: what is the link? Hum. Reprod. Update 2007; 13:313–327.
13. Carrell, DT, Emery, BR, Hammoud, S. The aetiology of sperm protamine abnormalities and their potential impact on the sperm epigenome. Int. J. Androl. 2008; 31:537–545.
14. Cheng, CY, Mruk, DD. The blood-testis barrier and its implications for male contraception. Pharmacol. Rev. 2012; 64:16–64.
15. Chevrel JP, editor. Anatomie clinique. Le edn. Hong Kong: Springer-Verlag France; 1994.
16. Cunha-Filho JS, et al. Physiopathological aspects of corpus luteum defect in infertile patients with mild/minimal endometriosis. J Assist Reprod Genet. 2003;20(3):117-21.
17. Dacheux, JL, Dacheux, F. New insights into epididymal function in relation to sperm maturation. Reproduction 2014; 147:R27–R42
18. Dauber W. Feneis. Nomenclatura Anatómica Ilus trada. Sa edn. Barcelona: Masson; 2006.
19. De Felici M. Origin, migration and proliferation of human primordial germ cells. In: Coticchio G, Alber-
20. De Wit, AE; Booij, SH; Giltay, EJ; Joffe, H; Schoevers, RA; Oldehinkel, AJ (2020)"Association of Use of Oral Contraceptives With Depressive Symptoms Among Adolescents and Young Women". JAMA Psychiatry. 77 (1): 52–59. doi:10.1001/jamapsychiatry.2019.2838. PMC 6777223. PMID 3157 7333.
21. De Ziegler D, et al. The hormonal control of endo- metrial receptivity: estrogen (E2) and progesterone. J Reprod Immunol. 1998; 39(1-2):149-66.
22. De Ziegler D, Pirtea P, Galliano D, Cicinelli E, Meldrum D. Optimal uterine anatomy and physiology necessary for normal implantation and placentation. Fertil Steril. 2016 Apr; 105(4):844-54.
23. De Ziegler D. Hormonal control of endometrial receptivity. Hum Reprod. 1995;10(1):4-7.

24. Egan ME, Lipsky MS (2000). "Diagnosis of Vaginitis". American Family Physician. 62 (5): 1095–104. PMID 10997533. Retrieved 7 July 2020.
25. Foti PV, Ognibene N, Spadola S, Caltabiano R, Farina R, Palmucci S, Milone P, Ettorre GC. Non-neoplastic diseases of the fallopian tube: MR imaging with emphasis on diffusion-weighted imaging. Insights Imaging. 2016 Jun;7(3):311-27.
26. Gartner LP. Color textbook of histology. Philadel phia: W. B. Saunders Company; 1997.
27. Gillman J. The development of the gonads in man, with a consideration of the role of fetal endocrines and the histogenesis of ovarian tumors. Contrib Embryol Carnegie Inst. 1948;32:81-131.
28. Gill-Sharma, MK, Choudhuri, JD, Souza, S. Sperm chromatin protamination: an endocrine perspective. Protein Pept. Lett. 2011; 18:786–801.
29. Girsh, E, Katz, N, Genkin, L, et al. Male age influences oocyte-donor program results. J. Assist. Reprod. Genet. 2008; 25:137–143.
30. Gray, A, Berlin, JA, McKinley, JB, Longcope, C. An examination of research design effects on the association of testosterone and male ageing: results of a meta analysis. J. Clin. Epidemiol. 1991; 44:671–684.
31. Guraya SS, editor. Cellular and molecular biology of human oogenesis, ovulation and early embryogen- esis: fundamentals, biomedical and clinical implica- tions in relation to infant disorders. New Delhi: New Age International Publishers; 2008.
32. Guthrie JR, et al. The menopausal transition: a 9-year prospective population-based study. The Melbourne Women's Midlife Health Project. Climacteric. 2004; 7(4):375-89.
33. Gynecology. (2015). Menstruation in girls and adolescents: using the menstrual cycle as a vital sign. ACOG Committee Opinion No. 651.
34. Hawkins SM, Matzuk MM. The menstrual cycle: basic biology. Ann NY Acad Sci. 2008;1135:10 8. 9. Achache H, Revel A. Endometrial receptivity mark- ers, the journey to successful embryo implantation. Hum Reprod Update. 2006;12(6):731–46.
35. Hecht, NB. Molecular mechanisms of male germ cell differentiation. Bioassays 1998; 20:555–561.

36. Iyer, V; Farquhar, C; Jepson, R (2000). Iyer, Vadeihi (ed.). "Oral contraceptive pills for heavy menstrual bleeding". Cochrane Database Syst Rev (2): CD000154. doi:10.1002/14651858.CD000154. PMID 10796696.

37. Johnson J, Bagley J, Skaznik-Wikiel M, et al. Oocyte generation in adult mammalian ovaries by putative germ cells in bone marrow and peripheral blood. Cell. 2005;122(2):303-15. doi:10.1016/j.cell.2005.06.031. PMID 16051153.

38. Johnson J, Canning J, Kaneko T, Pru J, Tilly J. Germ- line stem cells and follicular renewal in the postnatal mammalian ovary. Nature. 2004;428(6979):145-50. doi:10.1038/nature02316. PMID 15014492.

39. Johnson, L, Zane, RS, Petty, CS, Neaves, WB. Quantification of the human Sertoli cell population: Its distribution, relation to germ cell numbers, and age related decline. Biol. Reprod. 1984; 31:785–795.

40. Krausz, C, Bonaccorsi, L, Luconi, M, et al. Intracellular calcium increase and acrosome reaction in response to progesterone in human spermatozoa are correlated with in-vitro fertilization. Hum. Reprod. 1995; 10:120–124.

41. Lee, NPY, Cheng, CY. Nitric oxide/nitric oxide synthase, spermatogenesis, and tight junction dynamics. Biol. Reprod. 2004; 70:267–276.

42. Lessey BA. Assessment of endometrial receptivity. Fertil Steril. 2011;96(3):522-9.

43. Lessey BA. Endometrial receptivity and the window of implantation. Baillieres Best Pract Res Clin Obstet Gynaecol. 2000;14(5):775–88.

44. Lilja, H, Lundwall, A. Molecular cloning of epididymal and seminal vesicular transcripts encoding a semenogelin-related protein. Proc. Natl. Acad. Sci. U. S. A. 1992; 89:4559–4563.

45. Lotti, F, Corona, G, Maseroli, E, et al. Clinical implications of measuring prolactin levels in males of infertile couples. Andrology 2013; 1:764–771.

46. Machaty Z, Miller AR, Zhang L. Egg Activation at Fertilization. Adv Exp Med Biol. 2017;953:1-47.

47. Mahadevan, Harold Ellis, Vishy (2013). Clinical anatomy applied anatomy for students and junior doctors (13th ed.). Chichester, West Sussex, UK: Wiley-Blackwell. ISBN 9781118373767.

48. Masliukaite, I, Hagen, JM, Jahnukainen, K, et al. Establishing reference values for age related spermatogonial quantity in prepubertal human testes: a systematic review and meta-analysis. Fertil. Steril. 2016; 106:1652–1657.
49. Neaves, WB, Johnson, L, Petty, CS. Age-related change in numbers of other interstitial cells in testes of adult men: evidence bearing on the fate of Leydig cells lost with advanced age. Biol. Reprod. 1985; 33:259–269.
50. Netter FH. Atlas de Anatomía Humana. 4a edn. Bar- celona: Elsevier-Masson; 2007.
51. Nicholson, HD, Hardy, MP. Luteinizing hormone differentially regulates the secretion of testicular oxytocin and testosterone by purified adult rat Leydig cells in vitro. Endocrinology 1992; 130:671–677.
52. Obstetrics & Gynecology, 126, e143–146. Retrieved from https://www.acog.org/clinical/clinical-guidance/committee-opinion/articles/2015/12/menstruation-in-girls-and-adolescents-using-the-menstrual-cycle-as-a-vital-sign National Institute on Aging. (2017). What is menopause? Retrieved from https://www.nia.nih.gov/health/what-menopause
53. Office on Women's Health. Menopause basics. (2019). Retrieved from https://www.womenshealth.gov/ menopause/menopause-basics
54. Office on Women's Health. Trying to conceive. (2018). Retrieved from https://www.womenshealth.gov/ pregnancy/you-get-pregnant/trying-conceive
55. Wilcox, A.J., Weinberg, C.R., Baird, D.D., (1995). Effects on the probability of conception, survival of the pregnancy, and sex of the baby. N Engl J Med, 333(23):1517-21.
56. Oliva, R. Protamines and male infertility. Hum. Reprod. Update 2006; 12:417–435.
57. Paniagua, R, Nistal, M. Morphological and histometric study of human spermatogonia from birth to the onset of puberty. J. Anat. 1984; 139:535–552.
58. Paulsen F, Waschke J. Sobotta. Atlas de Anatomia Humana. 23a edn. Barcelona: Elsevier-España; 2012.
59. Peter, A, Lilja, H, Lundwall, A, Malm, J. Semenogelin I and semenogelin II, the major gel-forming proteins in human semen, are substrates for transglutaminase. Eur. J. Biochem. 1998; 252:216–221.

60. Public over, S, Harper, CV, Barratt, C. [Ca2+]i signaling in sperm—making the most of what you've got. Nat. Cell Biol. 2007; 9:235–242.
61. Puppo V. Embryology and anatomy of the vulva: the female orgasm and women's sexual health. Eur J Obstet Gynecol Reprod Biol. 2011 Jan;154(1):3-8.
62. Ragheb, AM, Sabanegh, Jr ES. Smoking and male fertility: a contemporary review. Arch. Med. Sci. 2009; 5:S13–S19.
63. Rastrelli, G, Corona, G, Maggi, M. The role of prolactin in andrology: what is new? Rev. Endocr. Metab. Disord. 2015; 16:233–248.
64. Revel A. Defective endometrial receptivity. Fertil Steril. 2012;97(5):1028-32.
65. Rimon-Dahari N, Yerushalmi-Heinemann L, Alyagor L, Dekel N. Ovarian Folliculogenesis. Results Probl Cell Differ. 2016;58:167-90.
66. Rode, B, Dirami, T, Bakouh, N, et al. The testis anion transporter TAT1 (SLC26A8) physically and functionally interacts with the cystic fibrosis transmembrane conductance regulator channel: a potential role during sperm capacitation. Hum. Mol. Genet. 2012; 21:1287–1298
67. Sammel MD, et al. Factors that influence entry into stages of the menopausal transition. Menopause. 2009;16(6):1218-27.
68. Scoullar, Michelle J. L.; Boeuf, Philippe; Peach, Elizabeth (2021). "Mycoplasma genitalium and Other Reproductive Tract Infections in Pregnant Women, Papua New Guinea, 2015–2017 - Volume 27, Number 3—March 2021 - Emerging Infectious Diseases journal - CDC". Emerging Infectious Diseases. 27 (3): 894–904. doi:10.3201/eid2703.201783. PMC 7920647. PMID 33622474. Retrieved 9 October 2022.
69. SEER Training Modules, Male Reproductive System, U.S. National Institutes of Health, National Cancer Institute. 27 April 2020. Retrieved from https://training.seer.cancer.gov/anatomy/reproductive/ male/
70. Sharpe, RM, McKinnell, C, Kivlin, C, Fisher, JS. Proliferation and functional maturation of Sertoli cells, and their relevance to disorders of testis function in adulthood. Reproduction 2003; 125:769–784.
71. Soules MR, et al. Executive summary: Stages of Reproductive Aging Workshop (STRAW). Climac- teric. 2001;4(4):267-72.

72. Sowers MR, et al. Anti-Mullerian hormone and inhibin B in the definition of ovarian aging and the menopause transition. J Clin Endocrinol Metab. 2008; 93(9):3478-83.

73. Speroff LF, Fritz MA, editor. Clinical gynecologic endocrinology and infertility. Philadelphia: Lippin- cott Williams & Wilkins; 2005.

74. Suzuki, K, Kise, H, Nishioka, J, Hayashi, T. The interaction among protein C inhibitor, prostate-specific antigen, and the semenogelin system. Semin. Thromb. Hemost. 2007; 33:46–52.

75. Tini DF, De Santis L, editors. Oogenesis. London: Springer-Verlag; 2012.

76. Tomar, AK, Sooch, BS, Singh, S, Yadav, S. Differential proteomics of human seminal plasma: a potential target for searching male infertility marker proteins. Proteomics Clin. Appl. 2012; 6:147–151.

77. Trainer, TD. Histology of the normal testis. Am. J. Surg. Pathol. 1987; 11:787–809.

78. Turner, RM. Moving to the beat: a review of mammalian sperm motility regulation. Reprod. Fert. Dev. 2006; 18:25–38.

79. UCLA Health Library, Los Angeles, CA." UCLA Health, healthinfo.uclahealth.org/Search/85,P00581. Accessed 19 Dec. 2020. "Polycystic Ovary Syndrome (PCOS): What Is PCOS? PCOS Symptoms, Treatment, Diagnosis |

80. UCLA Health. "Endometriosis: What Is Endometriosis? Endometriosis Symptoms, Treatment, Diagnosis – UCLA." UCLA Health, www.uclahealth.org/obgyn/endometriosis. Accessed 19 Dec. 2020. "Yeast Infection

81. UCLA." UCLA Health, www.uclahealth.org/obgyn/pcos. Accessed 19 Dec. 2020. "Fibroids: What Are Fibroids? Fibroids Symptoms, Treatment, Diagnosis – UCLA." UCLA Health, www.uclahealth.org/fibroids/what-are-fibroids. Accessed 19 Dec. 2020.

82. Waeber, C, Reymond, O, Reymond, M, Lemarchand-Beraud, T. Effects of hyper- and hypoprolactinemia on gonadotropin secretion, rat testicular luteinizing hormone/human chorionic gonadotropin receptors and testosterone production by isolated Leydig cells. Biol. Reprod. 1983; 28:167–177.

83. Woods NF, et al. Is the menopausal transition stress- ful? Observations of perceived stress from the Seattle Midlife Women's Health Study. Menopause. 2009;16(1):90-7.

84. Zaneveld, LG, Tauber, PF. Contribution of prostatic fluid components to the ejaculate. Prog. Clin. Biol. Res. 1981; 75A:265–277.

85. Zukerman, Z, Weiss, DB, Orvieto, R. Does preejaculatory penile secretion originating from Cowper's gland contain sperm? J. Assist. Reprod. Gen. 2003; 20:157–159.

www.ingramcontent.com/pod-product-compliance
Ingram Content Group UK Ltd.
Pitfield, Milton Keynes, MK11 3LW, UK
UKHW050750100325
4921UKWH00055B/1025